BUSINESS FUNDAM… …S

Streaml… …r
Opera…

DANI LOUISE SMITH

The Queen Of Business Organisation

Business Fundamentals

Streamline & Organise Your Operations For Success

By Dani Louise Smith,
The Queen of Business Organisation

First published in Great Britain in 2024
by Dani Louise Smith Via Amazon KDP

Edited by Louisa Herridge,
The Storytelling for Success Coach

Paperback ISBN 978-1-0686785-0-9
eBook ISBN 978-1-0686785-1-6

Printed and bound by Amazon KDP in Great Britain.

Contents

Foreword

Foreword, written by Lisa Lloyd-Jones

As I scrolled through Facebook one Wednesday evening, I stumbled across a girl with bright pink hair. I stopped the scroll to hear what she was saying. As I listened, I heard a familiar, warm Yorkshire accent like mine. I found that was the only similarity as I watched from a distance over the coming weeks.

Whilst I was nervous about social media, going live and organising my business, Dani was confident and determined with a steely look in her eye. She didn't give off the glossy fake vibes that I had seen before when looking at business coaches. She didn't promise that you would be earning a six-figure sum in twelve weeks. She was transparent and real. Truly real!

At the time she was working an employed job and running two businesses all whilst being a mum to three young children and wife to Dan, who I later discovered was disabled. I never once heard her complain. She set her goals and worked fiercely towards them. She shared her wins and her losses. She would adjust her strategy and continue towards her target. She would apologise when her young children interrupted her live streaming but showed that this was real life when you have a pre-schooler and you are working from home. Soon, she gave up her paid job as she knew that her passion was to help women in business just like her. I knew I wanted to work with Dani and the second she offered a paid programme, I was in!

She was half my age but brought energy and confidence that passed on to me. She was knowledgeable beyond her years and shared all the latest business strategies. She was kind and friendly, she knew all about the everyday challenges that keep us in procrastination (after all, she had more challenges than most). She could be sympathetic but also found ways to hold me accountable...and so my business grew and so did our friendship over the years. She has helped me to align, accelerate and automate my service-based business so that I now have recurring income which is more than I could have ever imagined when I started...and I know there is more to come.

Dani has stayed in her lane, not looking left and right. That's not to say her success happened in a straight line, there were bumps along the way, but she made tough decisions and emerged as the beautiful butterfly that is now known as *The Queen of Business Organisation*.

I always knew she would succeed because her systems were real and proven to work. Why? Because she has done it, lived it, known the struggle and created it herself. She's the real deal,

So, my friend (eek! I can call you that now) here is your book! You deserve your success; you have earned every bit of it. I can't wait to see what comes next for you, your lovely family, and your business.

Success has no limits!

Lisa Lloyd-Jones

Therapeutic Art Specialist Teacher
www.MindFullOf.Com
https://www.facebook.com/mindfullofartinfo

Founder of The Therapeutic Couch
Support community for parents of children and young people struggling with
additional needs and neurodiversity
https://www.facebook.com/groups/thetherapeuticcouch/

Introduction

This will be one of the greatest days of my life, but it hasn't happened yet. I can feel the vibration of the music through my body, as I move with it. I'm not alone, the whole room of people are in sync with the movements my hips make, mirrored arms raised as we hear the booming of the speakers echo into the hall. I'm dancing in front of people, with them following my random steps, just like I imagined I would as a little girl. My inner child is celebrating right now as she sees me teaching the moves to a song raising energy to a room full of women. Right there at the back is my husband and children, laughing but not mocking. 'She actually fucking did it,' they're thinking, not that they had a doubt.

We end this inspirational day with that big movement, in mind, body and soul, as a collective energetic shift within the room.

In this vision I have just hosted a sold-out masterpiece, a day event like no other, crafted carefully by me and my amazing team of talented women in business that I have connected with along the way. Bigger and better than I imagined, many leave to share their takeaways, the insights from the experience. Social media tags galore as they shine on the movement that this West Leeds girl, raising a family in Seacroft council estate, has created. It is a passion project, a vision, and a dream, to bring many together and connect like they never had before, to themselves, their goals, their businesses, and the world they found they could create.

I brought people into the room. They came to listen, watch, and learn and I delivered!

I hold a vision for where I can take this. Although this isn't reality yet, it's not the beginning or the end. The best is yet to come, but before we get there, I'm going to take you back. I will take you to where the vision started and I'm going to bring you on the journey with me, to become an Organised Business Queen.

I have wanted to write and publish a book since I could write. My inner six-year-old would be beaming with pride, and most likely dancing too, although I never could have envisioned, I would be sharing my knowledge and my own story publicly.

I came into the world in 1993, a September baby, the perfectionist, the organised one - a Virgo through and through.

I want to share with you a bit about why I'm writing this book today. Why organisation is massively important to me, and I believe it can be a game changer for you too. If you know me well, you will know that I often say I thrive in extraordinary circumstances, because it's true, I do. If you don't know me yet, then I would love to invite you to get to know me because there's nothing better than new connections on this business journey.

Compared to the average business owner, my family dynamic is somewhat far from average. The thing is though, we all have our shit to deal with. Nobody's life is perfect, things are tough sometimes and I wanted to start here.

I wanted to begin here because what's vital for you to know is that you can either sit looking at the shit life throws at you and boo hoo about it or you can do the opposite and make moves. Don't get me wrong, I used to have a 'woe is me,' mindset and hate the world. I often say I was a 'whiny kid' because I was. I developed that mindset in life, and it's taken work to shift it and takes continued work to not fall into old patterns.

We are all special. We all have our superpowers and I'm ready to share mine with you. I am *The Queen of Business Organisation* but I am also bloody amazing at thriving regardless of adversity, I don’t run a business based on circumstances, where I only show up when things are good; I show up for my business regardless and before I share the how, I want to take you into a glimpse of my life and why I'm the person to share what I'm about to share with you...

At this moment in time, I'm a thirty-year-old mum and wife. I met my husband young, got pregnant at nineteen, married at twenty-four. We have three children, all ten and under - that's a handful enough, right? We also have our boy, Koda; a mixed breed doggy and we have daily battles with multiple conditions and disabilities.

Thriving in Extraordinary Circumstances.

So, as I said, my life is complex.

Let's start with my husband, he is diagnosed with hypermobility joint disorder, arthritis, knee deformity, tremors, diabetes, and dyslexia. He is yet to be assessed for ADHD and autism, which I believe he does have and are often linked with dyslexia and hypermobility. These conditions affect his mobility and mental health, but he looks 'normal'. When you lift his trouser legs and sleeves of his shirt you can see scars from over thirteen surgeries, including a knee replacement at age thirty-four and frequent injuries to his arms from falls and other incidents, due to his conditions. If facing all this wasn't enough, we often get verbally abused on bus journeys, have on school runs or judged in many places, because of our age, his consistent use of crutches and believed to be 'faking it'. It's tough and it's why I advocate for not judging a book by its cover.

Then there's me. I have struggled mentally since I was a teenager. Anxiety and depression and in those teen years self-harm, but that, thankfully, is left way in the past. I'm managing on my own, without medication now, aiming for a holistic approach. I'm also overweight and it's affecting my body, with pain and I have plantar fasciitis, which can affect my ability physically on occasions. I have had to monitor my health for years, with a risk of hypertension. I have an unhealthy relationship with food and money and believe I'm undiagnosed ADHD. The way in which these affect my life is my focus, my impulses and shiny object syndrome, mindset, and ability to commit to daily tasks. Things such as cleaning or hygiene can be huge for me and other than saying it to my husband, this is the first time admitting to someone else. I used to start to believe I was lazy and had to be perfect to succeed and I'm glad today that now I know different. My mind just works in a different way, and I find the usual day-to-day things overwhelming.

My son, at the time of writing this, is seven. He is delayed with speech, socially and is awaiting autism assessments for a second time. We believe he is dyslexic, and we have daily challenges with him going into school and often school exclusions, meltdowns, and anxiety attacks, such as night terrors, bed wetting etc.

My other two children have no diagnosed conditions, but we do have anger from our eldest boy and lack of emotional regulation, I suspect due to our life and the challenges, which I often feel guilty for. Mum guilt should definitely be banned.

Then there is our girl, the stubborn baby of the household, but otherwise just as challenging as any other five-year-old.

When I write all this out it often shocks me. I question myself and see it and wonder how we manage all of it. The biggest win though is that my husband and I are a team, and we try to understand and support each other. We work together so that I can work from home and earn an income and so that he can rest and be cared for when needed. The dynamics have to work so that we withhold a family unit that supports our life as a whole.

It's not been easy, far from it. This is exactly why I must be on top form; I have to be organised, prepared, productive and resilient. I often see others not winning at business, not hitting desired goals, not earning, not thriving and it breaks my heart, but I also can see the gaps, because I started there. It's where I came from, negative mindset, life's curveballs and lack of money, lack of sales...these things we all have to face, no matter what stage we get to, and I only just learnt this lesson recently. The same things show up, just at a new level, but I always believe that if you prepare yourself in the best way possible you can survive. You can thrive. So that's the story I'm sharing with you and I'm going to teach you how to overcome adversity to thrive.

My business journey

My keepsakes business came first, taking six years before I made a substantial amount, I could actually do something with. The NHS job came just before that happened, as a way to make ends meet because of my lack of earning money from my business. Then I took on networking events and finally, I started earning money. I believe it was a combination of meeting new people and surrounding myself with like-minded people and the motivation it gave me but also the visibility it offered. It was here that I fell in love with all things business and supporting others to succeed.

I shared my story and started building connections. Then one day I came across a blog on creating a DMO: Daily Method of Operation. Apparently, it was a common network marketing term, and, in this blog, I discovered it was the list I had already created. I then shared this list, plus my content bank and other business tips that kept me organised, within the networking group and it went wild! My inbox flooded with business questions, people wanted help, people loved my methods. The DMO wasn't a new concept but the way I laid out my list and shared the spreadsheet was a game changer for many. Two of the ladies in that group told me I should teach this. I had knowledge and there were people ready for what I had. At first, I thought the knowledge was the things I learned from those free classes and networking, but I now know it's the way I do business differently, the systems I create, the ability to operate efficiently and save time. I then spent a whole month planning how I could become a business mentor and I launched on the 15th of January 2021, signing five clients on day one.

It was at this point that I was surrounded by a neurodiverse community online and followed an Instagram influencer sharing her ADHD traits and I resonated with nearly all of them. I recognised my anxieties and challenges with money, overwhelm with numbers were possibly that I am neurodivergent and as a result it has always impacted me, just not in the typical hyperactive and obvious way that you usually suspect. I now class myself as undiagnosed ADHD, as I am not pushing for diagnosis as I don't feel I need it. Organisation has become my coping strategy and all the work I have done on my mind, with therapy included has contributed to life being nearly manageable. I say nearly because as previously mentioned, my son is a SEN child, undergoing autism diagnosis and my husband has now been referred for both ADHD and autism. By the next time I write another book, they should hopefully both get their diagnosis. It's quite colourful in our house, the mix can be a challenge, especially the overwhelm all of us can get but it keeps life interesting, and we manage.

For many years it's been a battle of feast and famine. The long journey over six years, crafting a business from needle and thread and then deciding to teach my systems, processes and methods of business planning, strategy, and organisation. I want to make one thing clear, I am not teaching success from a point of making millions, because I am nowhere near that (yet!) but what I am doing is teaching from a place of balance, freedom and truly feeling aligned with my life every day I wake up. I have escaped feast and famine and grown a sustainable business model that allows me to earn a baseline income every month and predict my cashflow for months to come. What's a bigger achievement for me is the ability to do this for others.

Janice came to me as a face to face working therapist,

wanting to bring her business to the online world and impact more people. This is so aligned with my greater mission and so we worked together throughout a variety of modalities, on social media marketing, business planning and email marketing and now she has a thriving business, often with fully booked face to face sessions and running multiple online sessions plus creating passive income. It's a pleasure to see the efforts of the work that you teach blossom into such amazing results. I am so grateful to Janice, as she was the first client who told me exactly who I wanted to work with. I fell in love with the impact a holistic service-based business can have.

Lisa grew not one, but two businesses with me and I am so proud. Originally, we connected as she too ran a creative product business, making personalised gifts. A year into my coaching and mentoring journey, after working on her business, she approached me with a new idea. She wanted to become an art therapist and begin offering her services to support children with anxiety. After navigating our own son's anxiety, I was so inspired by her ideas and now two years later it is inspiring to see her action everything we work on together. Now booked with one-to-one clients, running local group sessions, and impacting the community by working alongside children and young people to make a difference to their lives. Succeeding with providing herself multiple income streams and sustaining consistent cash months and recurring revenue. Lisa has taught me that I am not the only one capable of juggling and leading a busy life, but one with passion and fulfilment and inspires me to continue to support more women in business to discover their inner Queen of Business Organisation.

Last but not least, I would like to bring you to my journey now. In three years, I have achieved so much and learned even more and continue to grow, with an inner knowing that what's to come is about building that extraordinary life I dream of.
In the last year I have pivoted my business and brought it crashing down (more on this later) then built it back up again, even stronger, whilst working less hours but earning more and achieving an income of over £5000 in one month, signing a £6000 contract over three months as an operations manager, selling out two group programmes and my one-to-one spaces. In this time, I have attended many business events, visited retreats, booked holidays, and ticked off many personal goals, including writing and publishing the book that you have within your hands today. Greater than this, the impact I have had I am so proud of. Helping others to earn a living doing what they love and achieving their own goals too just fills my heart with joy, which is exactly why Business Fundamentals has been created...

Throughout this book, I'm taking inspiration from my signature 12-month programme, 'Foundations' and paving the way for a step-by-step self-study and energetic, practical plan that you can implement, just from having this book in your hands. I worked with countless service-based business owners to start and grow an online business, using social media marketing, email marketing and networking as a platform for growth. As a qualified business enterprise and business foundations coach and mentor, life coach and qualified sales coach, I am equipped with the skills, but most importantly 11+ years of experience in online community building and business start-up and growth, having successfully run three businesses. I have helped clients achieve:

- Consistent four figures and beyond, in income per month and on the way to six figures annually.
- Launching a second successful business and signing contracts with local authorities.
- Exceed launch sales goals, with triple the numbers aimed for.
- Go from fully booked one-to-one clients, to creating multiple income streams and freeing up time.
- Creating consistent passive income after taking a face-to-face business online.

This book is going to be like taking a crash course in the fundamentals of business, but as The Queen of Business Organisation, I am going to ensure you start and grow a business whilst being organised and streamlining your operations. My aim, as you read this book, is to prepare you with the knowledge, resources, and tools to start and grow a successful business, with the foundations built to establish a strong brand, attract dreamy clients, and earn money, whilst doing what you love. I warn you though, nothing works unless you do. Be ready to make moves. Be ready to get deep into things you've never tried before. Be ready to push yourself.

Let's go!

Chapter 1

Clarity, Connection & Commitment

Life Analysis

When I first started my business, my overall mental health wasn't in the best place, so how could I practise stepping into a business mindset? The craziest thing was the conditioning from those around me that you must get a job and work hard, yet these same people were telling me not to legally notify our tax office of what I was doing and just take cash. I understand why but that narrative then sets a precedent of where you're going and that's not anywhere great if you begin with cheats and lies. It's not in my bones anyway and so I registered as self-employed, and I began this scary journey of being responsible for making my own money, on my own terms.

It's worth noting here that this isn't my very first business. At first, as a first-time mum, I had sewn a sock monkeys and begun selling them to my Facebook community (of which I grew to 8000+ without any social media training).

Those sock monkeys transformed into a keepsakes business, all handmade memorabilia and then that transformed into running networking events. From there I found a passion for teaching and that translated into becoming a creative business mentor until I fell in love with the digital marketing and service-based business world and transitioned into a business mentor for services, as *The Queen of Business Organisation*. As you can see, it's been quite a journey. This is all a symbol of how my mindset has evolved as I have grown and niched as I found my path with what I want to do.

Back when I started this business, I had succeeded with my keepsakes, making a consistent income, juggling life but I wasn't happy. I loved my work, but all other areas of my life were out of sync. I remember often hitting overdraft because I couldn't manage my finances. I remember the anxiety of facing it, having to get out of bed daily and face the world, then after a day of work, with family or socialising, whatever the scenario, I would tear myself apart, believing that others were talking about me, judging me and I was overwhelming myself with stories that weren't true and very little insight into what I could do about it. I was deep in depression and anxiety but nobody but my husband knew about it and so I continued to spiral and felt overwhelmed with everything I felt was beyond my control within my life.

Thankfully, I listened to a talk on money mindset, and it changed my life. The mental health aspect of my life got worse before it got better, but what is worth noting is that when my mind improved, my finances did too, my relationships did, and my children's anxieties did too.

Once I truly began my journey of building something I was passionate about and deciding to succeed with it and earn more money, I discovered that clarity played an important role, yet I didn't have enough of it. It was so clear that I wasn't connected to what I wanted out of life and so this presented a block. Knowing you want more but not knowing exactly what you want creates a confusion and unclear direction. You cannot get to your destination if you don't know the roads to get you there. This was something I massively had to work on.

The thing was, I could tell you I wanted something but the energy behind it was just a dream, not an understanding that it was possible if I decided it was and committed to it. This is the biggest difference between those who get what they want and those who don't, setting a clear intention and acting on it. I see it with goals and as a business mentor all the time and I feel power in always questioning and asking WHY, HOW & getting more INTENTIONAL. Having a VISION is the number one foundation for any successful business strategy.

Let's take some examples:

- I ask myself what I want to achieve in life in the next year. The answer, earn more money. Great, but why? How much more? What's the intention behind this and the significance of the change? The reality is I could earn just one penny more this time next year and I have achieved this desire, but is that *really* what I want? Nope. I want more than that and accepting, knowing this is okay too.

- I ask my client what her business goals are next month. Often in my mastermind, when creating a strategy, we set 3-5 focuses. My client said she wants to sell more of her masterclasses and grow her customer group. Instantly, my thoughts go to the lack of clarity here, already diminishing possibilities, because without a measurable outcome you cannot see a result, you cannot feel that happening, before it actually happens. At this point I push her to choose how many of the masterclass spaces she wants to sell and the exact number of people she wants to see in her group. Instantly the energy shifts, because once you know an action that has previously worked to sign one person up and get the sale, you then know how many more times to take that action to achieve the goal and so can continue to set that intention and achieve the goal.

I hope you can see the power of clarity, connecting to the desire with intention and taking action. Before moving on, deciding what you want and getting really clear on it, I'd like you to stop and rate the eight areas of your life right now. This is a task you can come back to, as your goals develop over time. Starting here gives an idea of what you need to work on right now. Sometimes we are financially abundant but lack creativity and so the goals to set are in this area, to work towards achieving balance. The key is to create a flow that aligns the eight life areas. So, let's begin there. Rate each of these areas of your life out of ten.

Ten being completely content.
One being absolutely out of alignment.

Career/Work/Business

0 1 2 3 4 5 6 7 8 9 10

Wealth/Money/Finances

0 1 2 3 4 5 6 7 8 9 10

Family/Friends/Relationships

0 1 2 3 4 5 6 7 8 9 10

Fun/Recreation & Creativity

0 1 2 3 4 5 6 7 8 9 10

LIFE SCORES

Health
(Physically & Mentally)

0 1 2 3 4 5 6 7 8 9 10

Love & Self Care

0 1 2 3 4 5 6 7 8 9 10

Personal/
Spirituality Development

0 1 2 3 4 5 6 7 8 9 10

Home/Physical Environment

0 1 2 3 4 5 6 7 8 9 10

Confusion to clarity

Now that you have done that exercise, you should be able to clearly see which areas of your life you need to give more energy to. This is one way to get clear on what your goals should be.
Within each life area, you can go deeper and become focused on what you particularly want. It's a great place to start and a book that helped me with this on my journey, with the contrast to clarity exercise featured in Michael Losier's 'Law of Attraction: The Secret Behind the Secret.'

In the book he explains that to understand what we really want, we first must look at what we *don't* want. When I read and completed this task it was very eye opening to how our human brains are wired to easily look at the negative and see what we haven't got or what we don't want in our lives. So, I began scribbling down my list. Everything I didn't want in my life, noted on paper in one of my random notebooks. Fast forward to just a few months ago, I discovered through one of my mentors, Samantha Hearne the effect of confirmation bias. This was the exact bias I had been experiencing, which was where you hold limiting beliefs so well that your mind looks to confirm them. Think about when you see a half a million-pound house, then check your bank, and confirm that your balance provides evidence that you cannot buy that house. Is that true though? Or is it biased? Think about this for a moment.

The reality is, it's *not true* that because your bank balance doesn't represent the full value of a house you desire that you cannot have it, but in fact what is true is the limiting beliefs held that you ‘never have enough’ and so your mind found evidence to prove so. In fact, it is possible, because you can put down a deposit, you can apply for a mortgage, and you can earn the money to buy that house. Whether or not the money sits inside your bank to take this action, the reality is that the confirmation you see isn't true and eliminates what's possible. How many times throughout our lives do we allow this confirmation bias to affect our overall actions, feelings, and experiences? This has a huge impact on your goals, your clarity around them and ability to achieve them.

In the book, Michael stated that once you know what you *don't* want it becomes clear what you do want, and I found this to be true. For example, I don't want to be in debt and on a low income. Knowing this made it easier to tap into knowing that what I actually did want was to be financially free and earn a higher income. This poses me asking the question of exactly what that looks like? Why? How much exactly? Then I can define a clear goal. Investing energy in what I didn't want allowed my thoughts to open to the opposite scenario of what I did want to see and before long my whole negative list of things I didn't want in my life became a long list of goals I was clear on and could get excited about.

Clarity isn’t clarity if you cannot measure it. Not everything has to be material but in business is it clear if it is tangible? If you decide that what you want is financial freedom, then what does that mean exactly? Spend some time to quantify it. Know your numbers whilst getting clear on what financial freedom will look like for you. How much will you need to earn to cover your business expenses, life expenses and have those luxuries? Clarity isn't just deciding what you want, it is actually being able to measure it too, so that you can then plan how that can happen. If you are clear on how many clients you need to get that figure, for example ten clients on a 121 basis, you can then take the next step of deciding the actions to take to sign those ten clients. Clarity with your vision as a starting point is just the beginning and it is absolutely and undeniably powerful.

I never used to set goals. I don't know why but I believe that it was possibly because people around me growing up never actively talked about what they wanted, other than my mum who is an active manifester and dreamer. She plans how she is spending money before she has it and I used to think it was ridiculous but now I know what I know I can see that it's just a vision and that as a starting point enables you to figure out the how. Now I live life by deciding what I want and then asking myself how I am going to make it happen, which nothing can happen if I am living daily in confusion, without enough clarity to take action. When I discovered what I wanted, it was actually to stop working so much that I burned out, after once upon a time juggling four job roles and knowing that busy-ness is not the life for me. I'm creative and so I enjoy doing lots of different things, but I knew that my life needed more flow. In recognising this I decided that I only want to work four days per week. Then I made that happen by organising my diary and setting that intention. I then decided that to fit in all my projects and manage my team and new ideas I would need a weekly admin day and content creation day, so I set the intention to work with clients only two days per week. I could physically see what that looked like within my diary, so I could measure how it works and change it if necessary. Clarity creates action.

The Triangle of Success

Once you know and understand exactly what you want, the commitment to it becomes easier. Looking at each area of your life, you can see where it needs more attention, using the clarity exercise you can decide exactly what it is you want and set those intentions.

This was a method I had been using for the last three years, until recently, when I noticed that I was still out of balance. My goals were exciting, and I would achieve more than ever but I still wasn't happy and there was a huge feeling of something 'missing.'

I believe in the power of putting yourself 'in the room.' This is where you surround yourself with others with similar desires to yourself so that your energy aligns, and you can gain so much from being around like-minded players in this game of life. I noticed rapidly that a lot of talk of energy was holding conversation and a recurring theme, be it the moon cycles, healing, menstruation, or feelings that were a topic of discussion and it brought my attention to the fact that there's is more than chasing wealth and to achieve true balance our energy needs to focus on health and happiness too: a Triangle of success.

What became clear is that wealth, health, and happiness were all something I wanted but my energy wasn't given to each area and so this resulted in physical and emotional pain, as I was treating my body and mind like they weren't important factors to achieve wealth. In my experience, this was in the form of abusing my body with trigger foods, that would swell up my throat, clog up my sinuses and affect my breathing. It was spending days sitting at my desk and not creating movement and so not only did my weight creep up, but my body began to create pain from what I believe is inflammation as my joints and muscles weren't getting what they needed. It was in the form of saying yes, overcommitting and overwhelming myself so I found myself in repeating patterns of working hours with no end. Eat, sleep, work, repeat. It wasn't healthy and although wealth wise, I did achieve more, I wasn't happy.

I'm a creative person and I crave time to binge watch the newest Netflix series, sit, and do some crochet with my favourite colour wool or spend my days off going on walks with my husband or for a cheeky quiet lunch whilst our children are in school. If that's what I wanted, why wasn't I consciously creating it?

We often do this, behave in a way that doesn't serve our higher self and fulfil our desires and purpose. It takes strength to break cycles, such as binge eating, staying slumped behind a screen at a desk and finding self-motivation to encourage a happier, healthier you but it all starts with a choice and a decision to. You have a choice to watch others achieve what they want or a choice to say YES to it for yourself.

Here lies where the balance can be created. The triad of success is about three focuses that align and impact each other. If you improve your health, you improve the way you feel, increasing productivity, increasing the effect of the work that you do and achieving greater results. In short, poor energy, poor performance, poor results. The triangle of the three becomes a cycle you can ride. Invest time in health by working with your energy, fuelling your body and movement will release happy hormones and offer the productivity to work on building your business and impact your wealth. Bringing in the money to achieve your goals, to pay off the debt, buy the hot tub or book the holiday, which will contribute further to your happiness. But how do we start this cycle before either exists? Feel healthier before implementing any exercise, be wealthier before the money arrives and have the happiness desired before commitment to the other two. Again, it's a choice. Choose your happiness to be what you've got. Create healthy habits with what you have and build wealth from where you are right now. Contribute to each in this way and see the evolution happen and greater balance in this cycle.

Once I was aware of this it changed the way I looked at life massively. I changed my schedule; I started doing more of what I love and working on what wealth looks like for me.

Let’s work on this for you:

- Where in your life do you need to work on your health?
- Where in your life do you need to improve wealth?
- Where in your life do you need to improve happiness?

Practical Action

Let's get you that clarity! Take a moment to complete the confusion to clarify the exercise and get really clear on what you do want. Look at your life scores in the eight areas to help you think about what you don't want in each area and the opposite being what you do want.

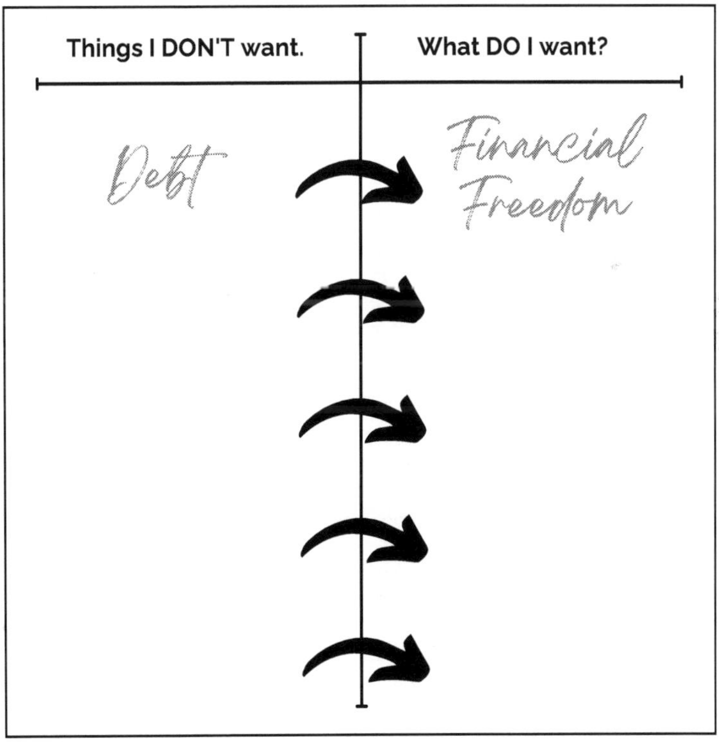

How does it feel for you to do this task?

As you write the things you do want, what limiting beliefs and inner chatter shows up for you?
Was it an easy task, or quite challenging?

The next step I really want you to focus on is finding the balance with all that you want from life and business. Complete an audit of these three areas:

- Health
- Wealth
- Happiness

	Health	Wealth	Happiness
How do you feel about this right now?			
What is working well?			
What could be improved?			

Now that you're clearer on what you want to achieve, you're in a place to start taking action!
Looking at your goals, map out actions for each of them. I recommend three to five things that you can do for each goal. Here's an example:

Goal: Financial Freedom: Pay off all my debts by May 2024

Actions:

- Analyse how much I owe and where, to gather overall totals.
- Analyse my income and expenditure to see how much I can pay off each month.
- Create a plan of which debts I will pay each month.

This is a goal I had and sitting down to look over my finances gave me back control and felt empowering. I started paying everything off rapidly once I had a plan in place that I was excited to execute, because I knew that doing so would set me free! The result was, I absolutely achieved it and paid off most of my debt by May 2024.

Look at your goals and start creating your plan:

Goal:

Actions:

Goal:

Actions:

Goal:

Actions:

Final note on taking action, because I know that you may need a reminder or need to hear it. No matter what is happening in your life, the things you cannot control, the unexpected circumstances you face, remind yourself of what you can control. You can control when and how you show up for your business. You are in total control of how you spend your time. You are in total control of the excuses you choose to use as reasons why you *can't* instead of reasons why you can or should. Never forget this.

Chapter 2

The Entrepreneurial Mind

Growth self-employed mindset

In my opinion and experience, there is a huge gap within the education system when it comes to finances and mental health. I find that there is not sufficient education to prepare you for real, raw adult life. We are taught where to go if we break a leg, we are taught equations and we are taught hygiene, but the things we really need, the things we should have available to us and the things that make the greatest difference, we are never given. Personal development and understanding money and self-sufficiency could change the world. Instead, we have lost souls dabbling drugs because of mental breakdowns, we have families in debt, and we have a mass of world issues. That's not where I choose to focus though, and you shouldn't either. Just because the real stuff we need isn't readily available, it doesn't mean we cannot find it.

When I started a business, especially after being employed

I needed my mindset to be completely different. I had to be focused on being self-led and taking action, because no manager or 'boss' was going to tell me what to do. On this entrepreneurial journey, many others feel the same. It took me a lot of time to realise this, even though my employed working life was only around ten years. I worked from age sixteen, fell pregnant at nineteen, had the baby, went back to work, and then started a business. It took me six years to make consistent money and to get paid regularly and consistently enough to be able to come off the benefits we were on. There are two factors that caused the situation to change, and they are mindset and strategy.

What you do in business and the success you have, or in fact with anything in life, is 80% mindset and 20% action, but let's not avoid the fact that you can do all the airy-fairy manifestation inner work in the world, but unless you get off your butt and do something then nothing is going to happen.

This is spoken from experience, as I was that twenty-one-year-old first-time mum, who started a business but was lazy in the action-taking department and it had to change.

I have always been organised in particular aspects of all my life and I'm not sure where it began really. Organising my craft drawers aged nine, organising the poker tournaments at work age eighteen… who knows? What I do know now though, is that if a problem arises, I literally plan my way out of it and that's what I am going to guide you to do.

If you're in a place where you're not taking action, I want you to ask yourself who is responsible for the success of your business? Start there and hold onto that answer for a moment. It is not your clients, it is not anything external, it is YOU. It is time to step up and get your mindset into that of an entrepreneur and what do entrepreneurs do? They make money!

The first step is to organise your mindset for success. The way I organise my mindset is by having a daily morning routine. If this work is new to you, I recommend trying everything and throwing everything at it.

My best advice around mindset is to be open, as this will pave the way for so much growth.
I want to support you to evolve with your new self-employed situation and to realise how different it is from being employed. In some instances, you have a similar narrative, in that you do need to show up daily, you do need to actively work, and you cannot just call in sick at the sound of a cough. In the daily action that will move you forward, this is where most aspiring entrepreneurs fail to show up and take action. It's too easy to adopt a mindset of 'I can just do it later.' Although running a business is different, you do need to show up every day and treat it like a non-negotiable job that if you don't show up for, you won't get paid from. This is in fact true, as you won't get paid if you are not doing the daily action that you need to.

Sit with this to adapt your mindset:

- How is running a business like having an employed job?
- How do you need to show up daily?
- Why is it important to your business that you are actively working on the business?
- Why is it important to not create excuses as to why you cannot do the work today?

If you ever find yourself stuck in a situation where you are not taking action and you're not sure why, come back to these questions and reflect.

At the same time, running a business and becoming self-employed is the opposite of being employed. The upside is that you can be totally flexible, work when you want to so that if you're a mum you can attend school class assemblies but be warned that flexibility can come with too much freedom and lack of action if you are not prepared and don't have a plan. This is where the self-employed mindset really has to be worked at as you need to be able to recognise that you hold the responsibility for everything within your business until you build a team and outsource.

You are the 'boss' and with that you become the marketer, the manager, the social media manager, the photographer, the personal brand, the web designer, the tech team, the bookkeeper and so much more. It is powerful to recognise this and to have the mindset that you are going to have to work more at the beginning and become all those people to get the results to enable you to grow. It's a lot to manage and a lot to master, but with the right resilient mindset you can apply yourself to it.

Sit with these and answer honestly to break and cycles that may hold you back:

- How is running a business the opposite of having an employed job?
- Who do you need to become to create success with this business?
- What behaviours do you need to let go of?
- What excuses are you making?

I couldn't write a section on the self-employed mindset without talking about excuses, because it was a pivotal shift for myself in my own businesses over the years. All the time I hear from business owners the same common excuses that they claim as reasons for not moving forward.

Mix those thoughts with fear, limiting beliefs, self-doubt and a whole life of conditioned stories and you are facing nothing but brick walls on your path. What if you can overcome those blocks, by simply climbing over the walls, or building a door and walking through? This is the perspective that you need to adapt to positively progress.

Which of these excuses have you made?

"I don't have time."

Time, it's relative. How you spend it is about choice and

priority. For example, you may say you don't have time to exercise but, in the evening, you spend two hours watching the latest Netflix series. I am not saying don't watch TV, we all deserve down time, but what I am saying is, it's about choice and priority. You have to open your mind to the possibility of creating the time to make that happen. This is a real-life situation, and I was using time as an excuse to hold me back from improving my health. What did I do? I started going to bed earlier, so I had only one hour of TV in the evening and then I started getting up earlier and using that extra hour of my day to exercise. I did it then so it was done first thing, and I couldn't use other excuses to get in the way of making it happen.

"I can't afford it."

Affordability. It is one in the same. Absolutely some people are in the most challenging of situations with money, no doubt about it. However, if you are buying that £30 weekly family take away, then can you really afford not to do the thing that will move you forward by offering the resources or the skills? Again, a real-life example. I used to believe I couldn't afford a lot of things, but the reality is, saving that £30 per week is not only good for my health, but also has a bigger return on investment if I save it up and buy the tech that I need, work with the mentor I know that can help me and climb over that wall to not allow money to become an issue. It's about recognising what you need against what you don't. I don't need a takeaway every week, it is nice to, and I haven't eliminated them completely, because just like watching TV, you deserve a treat, but the fact is, what I have needed in the past was to upskill to grow and make progress and I had to make that decision to prioritise that.

“I don’t know how.”

Finally, not knowing how. You can learn. Yes, it will take time, if time is coming up for you around this, read back to this whole section again and let that sink in. It doesn’t have to always cost money either. The beautiful thing about the internet these days is that you can learn almost anything at the click of a few buttons. Google and YouTube are amazing tools. I even have a whole range of videos on my own YouTube channel that are accessible, with hours of content with tips that will help you to lay down foundations that get you results. I know this because many times I have people make money without ever investing in me and just attending my live free training.

“It’s too hard.”

Lastly, this leaves you believing it's too hard. I am here to question that belief, more so because I had that when I was battling the tech years ago and feeling out of my depth, yet here I am doing it! If it was too hard, then how have so many people succeeded? It is not impossible and going back to not knowing the ‘how,’ you can learn.

This type of mindset work is ongoing. I always work on it because it’s too easy to fall back into old patterns of thinking. When I first set up my business, I had set a big goal to leave my job and the money wasn’t coming in, so I couldn’t make it happen. I actually needed to take action, because sitting around and watching TV or scrolling unintentionally on social media wasn’t going to bring in the sales. I was in the negative mindset that it was never going to work out, nobody wanted to buy from me, and I should give up. I battled these thoughts for years. I couldn't see that I needed to ask for the sale, that there were opportunities available to be visible and one day I did wake up and just decided that this year was going to be the year that things changed.

It was 2020 and at that time I had all the excuses not to succeed. When the pandemic hit, my husband's health got worse, which heightened my anxiety. We had a one-year-old, one of three kids, and I was working part time, juggling employment, business, and family. I had every excuse not to keep going, not to work on my business, not to do the daily actions that would move me forward, but instead I chose to work on it and in one of the toughest years financially for businesses, my first business skyrocketed and then I set up as a business mentor and coach. I didn’t build a business when circumstances were good, I decided to show up regardless and that’s the difference in the mindset of the person who succeeds.

Give anything a go to improve your mindset and I am going to help you take what you need and organise it into your life as a non-negotiable, because that’s exactly what it is if you want your business (and life) to be a success story. It starts with what your own inner thoughts are telling you and your beliefs deep down.

Money Mindset

Money is interesting. It holds so much power, yet it's just something that has the energy of exchange. It's not something we keep, or should intend to, because its existence is to be exchanged. The purpose of it is to trade, yet so many of us feel negative when we let it go. We feel so many emotions around not having enough and then mistakenly manifest more of it flowing away from us. Your money story can change and when I discovered this it was like a magic secret that I could play around with.

Whether you believe in the laws of the universe and manifestation, there's no denying that where focus goes, energy flows. Science proves that if you choose to think about something you're more likely to discover it in your reality. It's often that the thing we search for already exists, it's just that we are mindful of it. It's the same with money. This is why the mindset around money and sales needs to change if you desire to make more of it.

Discovering my money story was a huge eye-opener. Seeing how particular events had stored negative energy within me and instilled unwanted thought patterns that affected my reality was mind blowing. Think about your experiences with money; growing up, stories you absorbed by the media, things your parents said, friends said, it all contributes to your reality with money right now.

When I was eighteen, at a party, my uncle said in front of our entire family that I would be jobless, on benefits and with three children. At the time, these words angered me, made me feel embarrassed and humiliated. What I failed to notice then was that my subconscious would choose to hold onto them. So, my life played out in exactly that way. By the age of twenty-six I had three children, and my family were on benefits. I had allowed that narrative to impact my reality and an interesting thing happened. Once I was aware of the mindset and feelings around this story, I was able to change it. I started working on my belief to succeed with my business and I started working on my money mindset on a daily basis in order to let go of those feelings of shame and judgement. Within months I was earning enough money to come off benefits. I had intentionally shifted my focus and manifested the new circumstances into my reality as a result.

Of course, succeeding took action, to strategically work on my business, and it wasn't without the mindset behind it. Whether you believe you can or believe you can't, you're always right. So, whether you believe that money will flow to you or not you will have a connection with mind and reality. Learn more about this. Embody the energy of having money. See what happens. It's easier said than done, I know. The matter of fact is that this work is effective and that's why I'm going to help you organise your money mindset routine.

Money mindset is often negative and based on stories that you consume as you grow up. Everything you consume leads to your thought patterns and beliefs, which lead to actions. If your thought patterns are that 'money doesn't grow on trees,' then your belief becomes that money isn't easily accessible to you, which can result in the action of desperation. In many cases, this could present itself as putting your services on sale at a lower price than you would like to be paid, because of the money story that you cannot access it easily. This is similar to the belief that you have to 'work hard to play hard,' resulting in creating hustle to enable you to achieve the lovely things that you want.

I know of many people who work hard all year to pay for their all-inclusive holidays to spend a week living in luxury, only to be back to the daily grind again after seven days, but with a bigger laundry pile to shift through. In my opinion, working none-stop and burning out until that pre-booked holiday is unnatural for us to live as human beings. What if you could live life every day? Work a job you love, that doesn't feel like work, is within true alignment and have so much work/life balance that every week feels like a holiday. Think about the thought patterns that show up for you when it comes to money and how they become beliefs and transmit into the actions that you take.

- Recognise the thoughts you have around money.
- Recognise the beliefs you have formed around money.
- Recognise the actions you take with your relationship with money.
- Reflect on how you can change these thoughts, beliefs, and behaviours in the future?

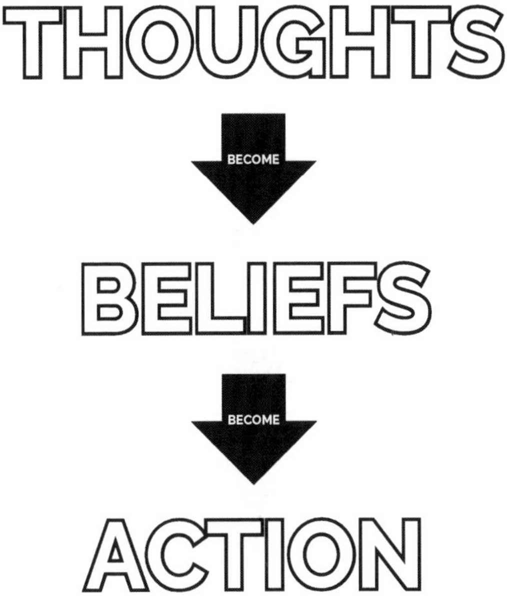

Beliefs, Fear & Failure

Belief is such a huge factor in the way you succeed and many of us feel the same inside. Have you ever felt unqualified or not good enough, and so belief in your ability to get what you want isn't within you? Imposter syndrome shows up and places you in freeze mode. You simply cannot sell the course you desire because then you will have to deliver it and then everyone will find out what a fraud you are. What if you challenged these thoughts and feelings and took the action? That's where your mind really steps into power because you're putting up a fight to succeed anyway.

I have felt this way many times due to beliefs that I'm not good enough and fears around failing. So many fears around failing. Failure to help people, deliver the service, sell it to anyone because what if?' I don't? I held onto the 'what if?' for so long that it became my reality. After experiencing being part of a mastermind, I quickly knew that it was exactly what I wanted to create, only to have the mindset monkeys convince me that nobody would buy my high ticket longer contract service, because I had never offered something like that before. My mind monkeys were right. I proved them right. I launched my very first mastermind, it did sell but it was totally out of alignment, and I wasn't profiting from it. The truth is, I felt such an imposter, selling a mastermind all about sales, when my business wasn't profitable. Hello imposter!

It took me time and a reality check to look at what I had achieved in sales so far. Was the successful product business that I had enough evidence that I did actually know what I was doing when it came to selling?

Many money mindset battles later, I stepped into creating an offer that I felt fully aligned with. *Sustainable Sales: The Mastermind* was born. I launched it but didn't sell any spaces. Not one client enrolled. It's not that I didn't have interest, it's that I wasn't delivering a message of belief in what I had created. Deep down I knew I had created something amazing, something that would have really benefited me on my journey, yet I wasn't succeeding in selling it.

At that point most business owners give up. I see it often that the fear of failing again takes over and the mind wins. However, determination and passion took hold for me, and I was ready to change the story as it unfolded. I worked on my mindset around the fear of failing again and decoded a belief that it was to become my signature program. I even increased the price, hired co-coaches, and worked on my beliefs around charging more money. Part of this meant that I had to work on the belief that it would sell at this new price. I sought guidance from my mentor at the time, growing my mindset and taking action on strategy. With confidence behind it, I launched, and I sold it. That launch was a pivotal point where my business not only became profitable, but it also was my first ever £8000 launch, the highest I had ever achieved at that time and a huge leap from my previous £3000 total sales launch.

Fear is something I now play with, especially after that time in my life, where I also jumped into a swimming pool even though I'm afraid of drowning. It gave me the sense to continue to face the fears and do it anyway. The reality is you never know if your beliefs, fears, and doubts are true until you test it out and the best feeling is proving them wrong.

I want to be transparent here though and share more insight to exactly what I was dealing with whilst succeeding with an £8000 launch and how mindset and fear can get the better of you and how I didn't allow it. I was launching in

September, six months after my husband had a knee replacement and moving house. Life had been pretty busy leading up to that point and then the start of the new school year presented huge challenges, in the form of my son refusing school, being excluded at least once per week, assaulting staff, having meltdowns every morning, running away from school grounds, running over roads and so much more behaviour I was unprepared to handle. He is awaiting autism assessments, again, second time referral after lack of evidence and no diagnosis previously. At that point I felt like my family circumstances were holding me back. How could a council estate mum of three, with so many challenges at home, succeed? My mindset dipped again. I had to fight to keep my faith and dismiss the beliefs that I would always be on benefits. It felt like I was jumping one step forward but being dragged two steps back. It was a battle daily in many ways, but I showed up regardless. Those challenges became my reason to succeed, so I could continue to work from home and be there for my family, instead of being forced into an employed job.

Let's face it, I don't like being told what to do and no employer would allow leaving work so often to collect your child because they were excluded again for abusing a teacher. It is what it is and it's not perfect right now, but I deal with it day by day. I could have easily chosen these challenges to become my excuses, but I didn't.

'I don't have time because I spent thirty minutes longer at school chasing my son in an attempt to get him into school'.

‘I can't do my work because my heads a mess after the school run.’

‘It will never work out because I will always be interrupted.’

Those were my exact thoughts, but I chose resilience. I changed the narrative, and I ploughed through anyway. My point here is to look at the challenges you're facing and eliminate the thought patterns that are excuses. Eliminate those beliefs that tell you that you can't. Eliminate the focus of anything other than a vision of you succeeding. I want your story to be one of winning. Thriving through adversity.

It gets to be easy as much as it gets to be hard all at the same time. Recognising your beliefs and having awareness is the first step, from then on it is about actively working towards changing them. It does take consistent practice. There are literally three steps to working through them:

- Recognise
- Reflect
- Realign

This method means to recognise what your beliefs are, and this could be around money, success, failure, or any other particular area that you feel your mind needs to work on right now. Once you have recognised your thought patterns and the beliefs that are within you, it’s about going deeper into where they actually came from in the first place. You cannot undo something that is instilled in you if you cannot recognise where the thoughts came from, or if they are even your thoughts. Take the example of my uncle embarrassing me in front of my family, it instilled a belief that I wouldn't be worth more than living on government funded benefits. Once I discovered this, it meant that I could then realign with what I actually wanted to believe. From there I worked on my new belief that being on benefits, having multiple children and being in a situation that I was in is okay. The system is set up to provide for you for a reason but at the same time having the ability to recognise that I wanted much more than that and working on the belief that actually I can have it.

Practical Actions

When I found myself with a need to work on my mindset, the very first thing I started to do was create space for myself before anything else in my day. I used to get out of bed when my kids woke up and end up falling into a day-to-day pattern of being mum, working, cleaning and the non-negotiables, but I wasn't putting my inner work first, I actually had no awareness that it was something I needed to do and when I discovered this, inside a book, I started getting up earlier each day and I begin a morning mindset routine. Disclaimer, it doesn't have to be morning and it doesn't have to be routine, as long as you're putting into practise something to work your mind like you would your body with exercise.

One of the things that has helped me on my entrepreneurial journey is journaling and so I invite you to grab your notebook and pen and use these journal prompts for your mindset around these areas:

Entrepreneurship:

- How am I being self-led as a business owner?
- How am I showing up daily and taking action?
- Where do I need to prioritise for my business to grow?
- What excuses am I making that are holding me back in building my business?

(Hint: often the excuses we have are that we don't have enough time, enough money or 'know-how' to achieve what we want)

Money:

- How do I feel about money right now?
- What are the stories around money in your past?
- What do you want your money story to be?
- What do I believe about people who have a lot of money? Is this true?

(Often, beliefs around those with money being 'rich bitches' or snobs crop up as the media portrays women with money this way. One of my favourite books, 'Get Rich, Lucky B*tch' by Denise Duffield Thomas opened my eyes wide to this!)

Limiting Beliefs and fear:

- Recognise: What beliefs are limiting you right now and what fears are showing up?

- Reflect: Where did these beliefs come from?
- Realign: What is the new belief that you want to adopt?
- What are my beliefs and feelings around selling?
- What are my reasons to succeed regardless of limiting beliefs and fears?
- If things don't work out, what's the worst that could happen?

(This was a powerful one for me, because in the worst-case scenario, I don't earn enough and go back onto benefits temporarily and that's okay! Sometimes you just need to release judgement around that!)

Now that you have done some inner work and thought deeper around some of these mindset challenges that many of us business owners face, it's time to prep your mindset routine. You may have heard this recommended before, or even have tried it before but did you stick to it for three weeks or more? It takes three weeks to form a habit and only then will you really reap the benefits. I have to admit, I have been up and down in consistency with my morning mindset routine, but I do really believe in it and know that my productivity and energy increases when I do it.

Let's begin with a brainstorm. Map out the things that you would like to include in your mindset routine. Here is my example:

When you implement your mindset routine, it doesn't have to be in the morning, it doesn't have to be at bedtime, it can be any time of day that suits you best, any order and any activities that work for you. Here are some recommended actions to take that will help with your mind and physical health:

- Hydrate before caffeine. Drink water before coffee. If possible, have coffee after eating.
- Move. Whether it's just a five-minute dance, fifteen-minute yoga or a full thirty-minute workout, including movement will shift energy and make you feel good as you release endorphins.
- Breathe. Doing some breathwork acts as a great mindful reset for your body. Allow it to really take in oxygen.

- Connect. When you have desires and goals, it's always great to remind yourself of what you're working hard for. You could connect with visualisation or writing your goal down. Writing a goal down on paper is 47% more likely to manifest and backed by a plan it is 80% more likely, which is why I am going to help you with strategy later in this book.

Here are some things you could try:

- Journaling
- Meditation
- EFT (emotional freedom tapping)
- Hypnotherapy
- Counselling
- Coaching (on life/business)
- Affirmations
- Motivational talks/podcasts
- Other therapies

Once you have your mindset routine mapped out, all you need to do is plan it into your diary, set an alarm and implement it. Enjoy!

Chapter 3

Planning & Preparation

Product suite & marketing mapping

Now we have done the mindset and goals work, let's get down to business. Here lies the biggest challenge business owners face, either having so many ideas and wanting to do them all or not knowing where to begin. It's so common and you're not alone but the reality is you just cannot do everything at once. So, here's where to begin…

I love a good brainstorm. Get your paper and coloured pens. If you're creative like me this is exactly how you will do it. Start writing every product idea you ever had. Write everything that you ever thought of selling. Although you won't do all these right now, it's useful for forward thinking.

When I wrote out my product suite in 2023, I discovered that I had a huge gap. I offered loads of free stuff; some high ticket offers and one low ticket but nothing in between.

In my product suite low ticket is anything under £49 and high ticket is £1000+. For you it may be higher or lower, depending on your business and price range.

In-between both low and high, I call this the mid-range. It's an opportunity for others to have access to you that doesn't offer as much as your one-to-one service might, things such as a masterclass or download.

Now you may come up stuck if you're a new business with only one service and its low ticket, so I want to support you to think outside of the box. For example, I had a client who was launching a children's book. Very new to the business world, it was her first and only product. Other than the collaboration book she had been part of, how could she build a product suite?

Here are questions I asked:

- What skills do you have that you could teach?
- What knowledge do you have that you could offer to your customers?
- What problems could you help solve?

Once answering these, it became very clear what could be offered, to provide a selection of offers at different price points.

She had writing skills, which could be taught in the form of a course, which became her mid-range offer, but also available as a 121 offer too. She had knowledge of writing and publishing a children's book, so she added a masterclass for this to her product suite too. The problem solved with her original product was bringing families together during a busy lifestyle, so they had quality time, which is where her children's books came in, as a low-ticket offer.

Answer the above questions for yourself and see what ideas you generate whilst you brainstorm. I always take at least three to five of my offers and map them out onto my product suite triangle, so I can clearly see what I'm offering for the year ahead.

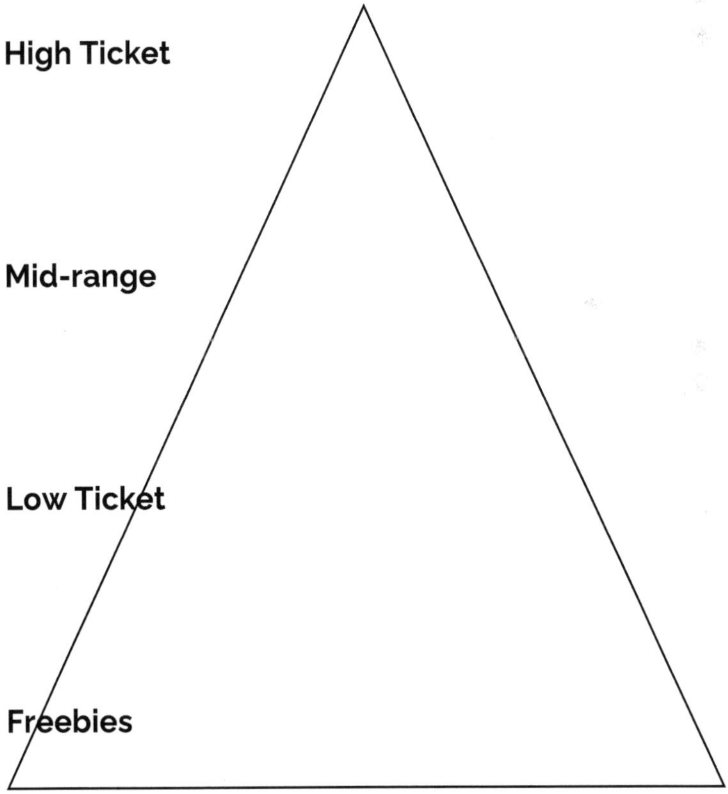

Once I decide on exactly what I am going to be selling I then plan for what I'm going to sell throughout the year e.g. January I may focus on a low-ticket offer, February a group course, and March a high ticket.

Here is an exact example of one of my plans:

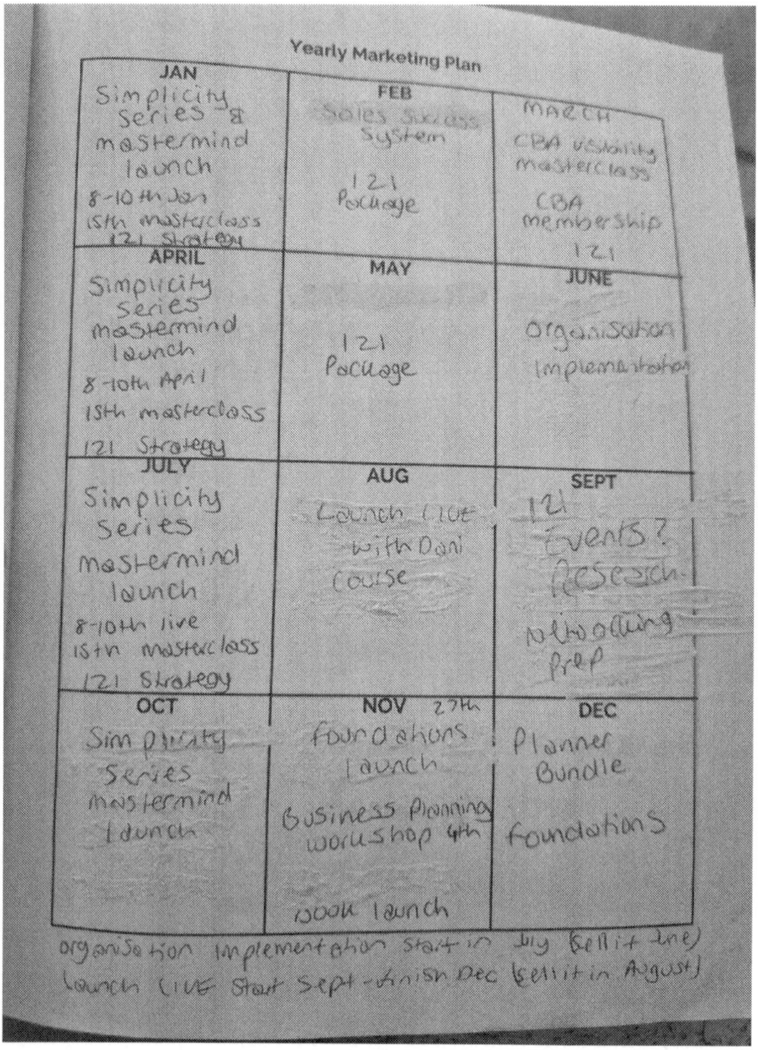

Yearly Marketing Plan

JAN	FEB	MARCH
Simplicity Series & mastermind launch 8-10th Jan 15th masterclass 121 Strategy	Sales Success System 121 Package	CBA visibility masterclass CBA membership 121

APRIL	MAY	JUNE
Simplicity Series mastermind launch 8-10th April 15th masterclass 121 Strategy	121 Package	Organisation Implementation

JULY	AUG	SEPT
Simplicity Series mastermind launch 8-10th live 15th masterclass 121 Strategy	Launch LIVE with Dani Course	121 Events? Research networking prep

OCT	NOV 27th	DEC
Simplicity Series mastermind launch	Foundations launch Business Planning workshop 4th book launch	Planner Bundle foundations

organisation implementation start in July (sell it June)
Launch LIVE start Sept - finish Dec (sell it in August)

Give this a go for yourself:

MARKETING MAP

JAN	FEB	MARCH
APRIL	MAY	JUNE
JUL	AUG	SEPT
OCT	NOV	DEC

It helps to have clarity around what you're selling when creating a map of direction that you can use to support your overall goals and stay organised with. A lot of business owners don't like to do this in fear of restrictions, but I'll let you know a secret, this is YOUR business, and you can change your plan at any time. In fact, you will see from my own plan that tippex was used as I changed my focus with a particular service I was offering. I eliminated it from my product suite because I wasn't aligned with it anymore and it's so important to connect with what you're selling. If the offers you're creating are something you can be excited about then you're more likely to get greater results. Keep this in mind when mapping out what you will be marketing over the year.

I want to share with you the story of the first service I ever launched with this business and exactly how it was so successful straight away, because I often see business owners get an idea, create it, launch it and nobody buys so they feel disheartened. My first ever service as a mentor and coach was an affordable £15 membership. On day one I welcomed five clients. It was amazing as I had literally launched my business that exact day, on 15th January 2021. I had no big email list or active Facebook group, I just planned a month before; to advertise a five-day challenge, I delivered it and on that launch day I attracted my first client just seconds after my first email went out. Here's this thing, on the outside it looked really successful, it's rare to launch a brand-new business and welcome in five paying clients straight away. I want to share the real truth behind how that happened. The keepsakes business had been wildly successful the year before and I had been connecting with creative business owners that whole time, networking and building awareness of who I am. Although I was very new, launching as a creative business coach, my network seeing the success I had in my own creative business generated enough credibility and trust built for people to pay money to work with me. Although my actual plan and work only took one month, I had actually been building a ready-made audience for years without knowing it. So, the next time you create an offer, and the result isn't quite what you wanted, remember this. It takes time to nail your offer, to connect with the ideal clients, build your network and build the like, know, and trust with those people.

From that day on I then became a business mentor and coach.

Planning to Plan and Productive Intentions

This one thing that was a game changer for my planning and productivity was 'Planning to Plan.'
The thing is most business owners don't 'have time' to plan and that's why they're not doing it. The first thing I want you to do here is eliminate the excuse that you don't have time. Instead, let's look at making the time. When it comes to time management and productivity, it's always about priority rather than the reality being that you don't have time. I see this coming up all the time for my clients and audience. I have a question to ask though, **do your goals and dreams matter enough to you for you to prioritise what you need to do for them to succeed?** Read that again. Let's face it, you're more than likely not achieving if you're not leading with what you want, which is why a whole chapter of this book was dedicated to clarity and goals and I talked a lot about time and excuses in chapter two.

It's time to start prioritising the things that will move your business forward.

Planning is something I love to do, and I know that it doesn't come naturally to everyone and that's OK, you just need to find a way that works for you. When I first discovered time management it was all about time blocking every thirty minutes and that's less than ideal or suitable for everyone. Your first 'to do' is to decide when you're going to plan.

- When are you planning/setting your goals?
- When are you planning your actions?

You absolutely need to find your own way, but I will share my exact method of planning with you:

1. I spend time each month planning my goals, actions, and strategy. I include my mastermind clients in this too.
2. I spend time each month planning my content.
3. I spend time each week revising where I'm at, recent wins and then plan my actions for the week ahead.
4. I spend time daily revising my day ahead and setting intentions.

It's a lot of planning... but it works for me!

The key though is to plan but ensure you are also acting on those plans too. I know that some entrepreneurs find this a challenge, especially those with ADHD and time-blocking is often the go-to recommendation for anyone finding time management a difficultly. I believe that time-blocking doesn't work for everyone. Sometimes it does work for me, then I get bored or overwhelmed and it doesn't and so I adapted based on this, tried, and tested myself and now explore my ideas with my clients. If you find time-blocking by hourly increments difficult, then this next tip is for you; I always recommend instead to block a focus per day and so it becomes easier to take the required action, as it feels less overwhelming than hourly increments set out over the day.

Let's also talk about productive intentions. Backtracking to those goals you were setting and getting clear on in chapter two, ask yourself:

Are you really taking productive action that's aligned with making those goals happen?
Being productive is 'achieving a significant amount or result.' This only happens when you are clear on the actions you need to take.

When I started my first business, I wasted a lot of time staring blankly at my phone every day, trying to materialise content to share on my pages. I had no idea at all what to say or do and so sometimes not only did I waste time, but I then skipped doing it, took no action and here lies inconsistency. This wasn't getting results. What happens when you 'wing it' is less focus, lack of strategic action and the energy behind it impacts the result. I understand that, in this case, you can't be intentional with content if you don't know what to say and post. The thing about this is, you can learn. I did learn, eventually. Any time you find yourself in a mind block, unable to take action and procrastinating through lack of clarity, go and learn the thing and then implement the thing. You can do a lot of this for free or at a low cost in books like this. Once you know what you need to do, you can be more intentional and as a result, more productive with your time. Often lack of productivity is presented via procrastination, as a result of fear and anxiety, often present with ADHD. I have certainly been no stranger to this. The more clarity you have and coping strategies implemented, the easier it becomes to eliminate overwhelm and those recurring bouts of fear and anxiety that lead to procrastination.

When I became a business mentor, I was also a keepsake maker, with a book full of orders, I was running popular networking events in person and holding down a sixteen-hour part time job at our local hospital, plus ten hours per week travelling time. I had to master my time in order for all of this to work and be profitable, around family life. I don't recommend having four jobs, but we were desperate for money, hence the employed work and I was passionate about my businesses. I would have never succeeded if I hadn't organised my plans on a weekly basis.

In 2021 I set the goal to leave my part time job and that happened because I was able to make my new mentoring and coaching business profitable and was brave enough to take the action and leave. It was a lot to handle, but through planning my working day efficiently I was able to maintain making over ten memory bears per week, working with clients on their businesses and running networking events. I was running three active online Facebook group communities and profiting from them all. Nothing is impossible if you are passionate about what you do, it truly aligns with you, and you have a plan.

Sort Your Schedule

One of the most challenging things about entrepreneurship versus an employed job role is that nobody tells you how to use your time. When you have a job, you know how you're spending your shift and the action you need to take. Let this be said that if you're currently winging it then I want that to change from this point on. I'm going to be honest with you, if you continue to wing it and don't intend to plan at all then you may as well throw this book in the bin. I don't mess around when it comes to business planning, as I know how powerful it is, I'm proof of how powerful it is, and the most highly successful businesses have a plan.

What I'm not stating though is that a plan is set in stone and midway you cannot adjust and pivot because you absolutely can and sometimes it's needed. I'm guessing you picked up this book to get help to be more organised and not just dance around the idea, right? Yes? Great, now let's really start making a difference.

I want you to visualise your dream schedule. I know that for you it may be a long way off yet, whilst you're still tied to a 9 to 5, or your children are young. I totally get this, my children are age ten and under at the time of writing this, so school runs are a non-negotiable part of my own schedule and of course my dream isn't to be doing school runs. Realistically I *could* outsource them, but I also know that I don't want to and love to be there for that part of the day for my children, even though it's often, okay daily, quite stressful. For many years my SEN son has had challenging behaviour and leading to consistent school exclusions. Not one part of this is my dream, but it is life. I accept it and know that it has an impact on my dream schedule.

This is just one of many factors that will adapt your dream. Once you have mapped out that dream schedule, adjust it based on your current needs. One example might be, that your dream schedule is working four hours a day on your business, but you currently have an employed job. That's okay, you can create your dream schedule and your 'for now' schedule, with your aim to work towards building your dream schedule, with small changes.

Okay, so let's get practical about what your dream schedule needs to include. Here are some steps and ideas to map out your dream schedule:

1. Brainstorm everything you need to do to run a business, a home, work your job, be a parent or care for your pet or loved ones. Don't forget yourself!
2. Take note of things you're currently not doing that you would like to do. For me, it was writing this book.
3. Aside from each of your tasks on your brainstorm, allocate a time and frequency. How much time does the task take and how frequently do you need to do it?

I prioritise exercise, as it's important to work on your health, self-care, such as hair care, skin care or doing something that aids my mindset growth related that helps me release stagnant energy and makes me feel good, often creative activities that I enjoy doing and feel desire to do.

Here are some examples of things on my list:

- School run thirty-minutes at 8.30 am & 3.00 pm Mon-Fri (non-negotiable.)
- Content creation three hours on a Monday, weekly (business.)
- Bookkeeping one hour monthly (business & finances.)
- Zumba three hours including travel, weekly on a Monday (Exercise, self-care & desire.)

Now that you have an idea of what your dream schedule could start to look like, start to create it. I recommend a visual that you can see and use every week as you plan out your week ahead. I use it on a Sunday to reference where I'm spending my time. I love to colour code mine too!

Here is my example:

Weekly Schedule

Time	Mon	Tue	Wed	Thu	Fri
7:00	Morning Routine	Morning Routine	Morning Routine	Morning Routine	Morning Routine
8:00	School Run	School Run	School Run	School Run	School Run
9:00	DMO	DMO		DMO	DMO
10:00	Content	Adhoc work		121 Client	121 Client
11:00	Content	Adhoc work		Mastermind	121 Client
12:00	Lunch	Lunch	Lunch	Lunch	Lunch
13:00	Mastermind	Adhoc work		121 Client	121 Client
14:00	Content	Exorcise class		121 Client	121 Client
15:00	School Run	School Run	School Run	School Run	School Run
16:00	Housework	Housework		Housework	Housework
17:00	Dinner	Dinner	Dinner	Dinner	Dinner
18:00	Zumba				
19:00	Zumba				Family Movie

Here is my example:

Schedule Notes

Mon

Attend AM MIB networking session once per month.

10am /4pm session with my mentor every 2weeks.

No Zumba on bank hols.

Tue

1st week every month call with Fi.

3rd Tues every month meet for co-working with Amy & Fi.

Every 6 weeks, 4hr in person client session.

Wed

Day off.

Last week of month therapy with Neena.

Thu

10am 2nd week of every month, Foundation group program.

Book keeping first week every month.

Fri

Attend networking or business events if no clients in.

Once per month associate coach session in mastermind.

Sat

Day off.

Sun

Day off.

Plan for week ahead.

Notes

Last week every quarter, week off.

Here's a template for you:

Weekly Schedule

Time	Mon	Tue	Wed	Thu	Fri
7:00					
8:00					
9:00					
10:00					
11:00					
12:00					
13:00					
14:00					
15:00					
16:00					
17:00					
18:00					
19:00					

Here's a template for you:

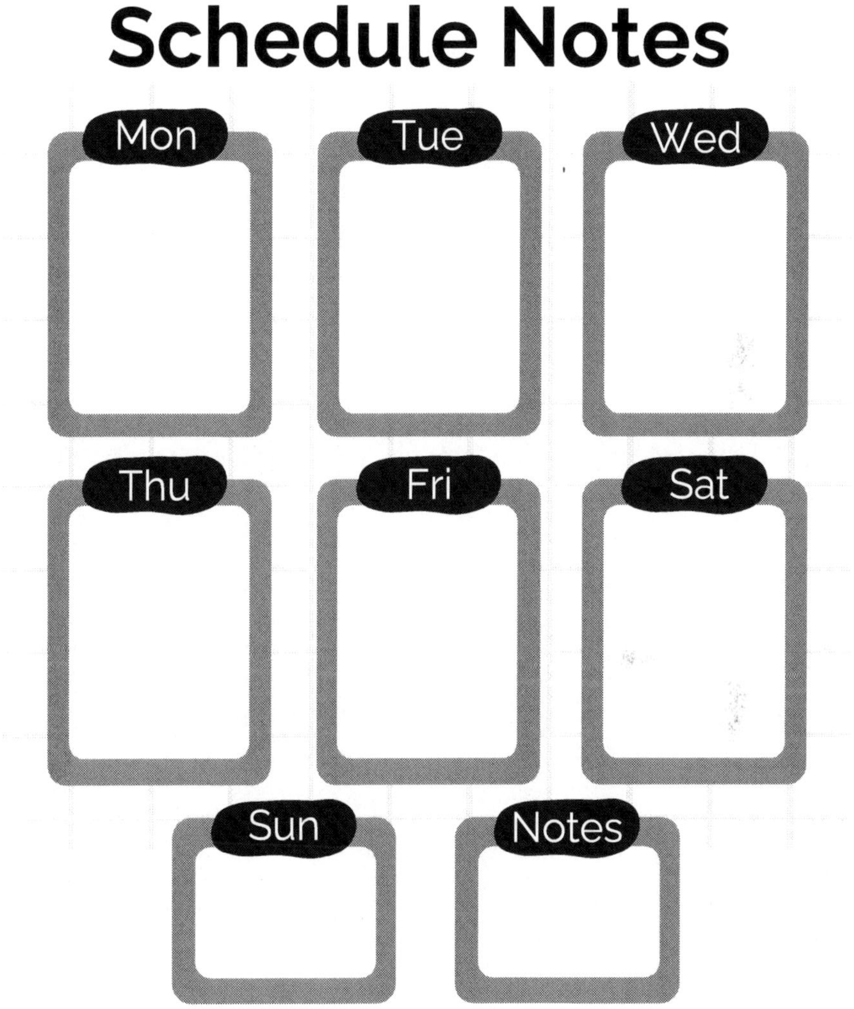

When you start implementing your new schedule, recognise how it feels for you. When I had those four jobs, I was sleeping away my weekends from being so exhausted and burned out. It is not attainable, and I see way too many business owners falling into the trap of not managing time well, always chasing their tail and overworking, leading to the exact same situation I was in.

In 2021 I handed in my notice at work and the instant freedom I felt with having an additional twenty-six hours per week was amazing. It felt so good but as I was used to working so much, I fell into a trap of filling every space inside my diary and overworking again, especially once my kids were back in school after summer. At that moment in time, I set a goal to have a midweek day off and only work four days per week. My schedule wasn't working with me, instead it worked against me. I was juggling two businesses, after all. I made adaptations and created set days where I would work on each business. Mondays were for making, I would be sewing loads of bears for families across the UK. Tuesdays were my catch-up days, where I would pick up any overflow for each business and Thursdays and Fridays became my client days. I arranged the networking events around this new schedule, and it was working really well, until it wasn't.

Preparation & Practical Steps

For this last section of this chapter, I'd like to review what I have covered and give you a checklist. I'm creating this to keep you moving forward after all.

Your checklist:

- Brainstorm services you could offer.
- Plan out your product suite.
- Create a marketing map.
- Plan in time to plan.
- Create your dream schedule and your 'for now' schedule.

Another handy tool is my phone alarms, I use these to remind me of activities that take the extra push, such as interrupting a hyperfocus work task at 3 pm so I can go do the school run. Having this is a godsend because I am the mum that would turn up late after paying no attention to the time. With my own challenges with hyperfocus, potentially undiagnosed ADHD, restricting time limits on tasks to keep focus and having alarms and reminders is effective, because I get very distracted by noises, movement and interruption whilst also finding sitting in one spot a challenge, it's quite a juxtaposition. This can bring me into overwhelm and procrastination, so finding coping strategies has been a godsend.

Product suite and different offers at different entry points, so that there is a way to work with you at different levels is super important for a sustainable income. Take note though, if you had lots of amazing ideas that didn't make it onto your product suite for this year, then keep them saved for later.

Marketing map to ensure you are utilising are setting yourself up to market your services in the best possible way for you. Having a clear direction, aligned with your overall financial goals can contribute to the celebration of achieving them.

Planning. At this point you should know how essential I believe this is. If you're screaming at me all the excuses because you cannot right now, go back to chapter one. You need to work on your mindset then take action.

Now that you've done some planning, I don't want you to forget about it. Anything that is a recurring task you could set reminders for. I personally use Google calendar and have EVERYTHING in there. I especially love that on Tuesdays, in my 'ad hoc' block I can add a checklist in the description of the event I've set up, so each week I have productive intentions.

Enjoy implementing your new organisational planning methods, but tweak as needed.

Top tip! Plan in some time to read the rest of this book and implement the tasks. You will thank me for this later!

By this point, achieving the goal of leaving my job, as organised as I had become with my time, I felt out of alignment with all the work I was doing. Although my businesses were both in profit, I was spending (investing) a lot of money, over £10,000 in a year on training, coaching and development and a lot of time, working long days with 6 am starts and 11 pm finishes. I invested in my first ever mastermind, a £2000+ investment, which was big and scary. I had never paid so much money to work with a business coach and a group of strangers before. Those strangers very quickly became friends and even to this day I work with some of them within my business. In that group I formed a business bestie relationship with Fiona Green, who is now my copywriter and the expert sales copy coach inside my mastermind. I met Gemma Holden, Mrs. Mindset, who is also an expert mindset coach inside my mastermind. I formed a stronger relationship with Carly Murphy, who at the time was my manifestation coach and these days she is my tech expert, dealing with everything tech behind the scenes of my business.

I met many amazing women I have connected with and worked with in many ways and inspired me to set a goal to leave my employed job. The reality was, I was making a lot of money, but spending it rapidly and racking up debt, although I didn't need to, because I was earning a lot. Looking back, I realise I couldn't handle all the money and how busy I had become. The burnout was weekly, it was making me regularly ill, especially as I was doing all the mindset work but nothing physical to help my body.

Two years into full time self-employment I started realising the build-up of stress, teamed with the guilt of wanting to quit. If I gave up on something I had done for so long, I felt like I had failed but the truth was that I just wasn't aligned with my first business anymore. I was making a lot of money with a high demand and great reputation, but prices of supplies went up, it was time consuming, and a lot of people didn't value or appreciate the skill and time of handmade work. In June 2023, exactly two years after handing in my notice in my last employed job, I announced the closure of Danique Keepsakes and that I would be focusing on mentoring full time. It was one of the hardest decisions I had ever made, after ten years of work but the keepsakes business was a huge part of my journey, I learned a lot and love that it took me to where I am now. I found a passion for running a service-based business and the alignment meant everything. You have to love what you do, fully, otherwise the lack of passion and ease around it will continue to bring up blocks within your mind, body, and soul.

Chapter 4

Branding Buster

Introduction to Branding

If I ask you what a brand is, do you really know? Most people think of logos, colours, fonts and maybe even the music that the ads play on TV. It all does play a part in your branding but there is so much more than our senses can see and hear. The way we consume a brand is about all that stuff but also a message, a unique selling point and clarity on who you are and what you do. Communication plays a huge factor in the success of your business, and it begins here, a clear knowing of your brand and your values.

The visual aspects of branding are easier to organise. You can design graphics on apps like Canva and even design a quality logo too. I recommend designing a brand kit to get started. I actually have many, for different projects.

A brand's positioning and message is something entirely

different that can really make or break a business. When a client is mid-launch and the service isn't selling, I always recommend starting by going back over the brand positioning and message. This is the key, no matter how big or small an audience you're connected to.

A brand's positioning is a statement of why you are different. In marketing, this is known as your unique selling point (USP). In today's world you need to clearly understand this, to set you apart from competition and connect to your ideal clients. There are many people out there that offer what you do or do similar and so you need to stand out from the crowd.

My brand positioning involves two key phrases when I introduce myself and share what I do, because they create interest and want to know more.

- Thriving through adversity.
- Showing up for my business regardless of extraordinary circumstances.

These two phrases instantly have people wondering the adversity I have faced and what these extraordinary circumstances are and so I share a snapshot of this. Why? Well, this positions me as the go-to business mentor if someone is also building a business but facing similar challenges in life. I create the 'proof' that you can overcome it and succeed. This positioning, along with my message, creates inspiration and desire. People tell me all the time they 'wish they had my courage/strength/power/

organisation.'

This is exactly why I began this book talking about this as my superpower, because before you take action and read my book, you need to understand how I am the go-to for business organisation and helping you earn money with an online business even if you are facing adversity. The reality is a lot of people face adversity and starting a business can be one way to overcome it.

Brand message is about taking your USP and going deeper into what you do and how you make this true.

Look at my business, for example. I'm a business mentor and coach. There is a lot of competition out there in this industry right now. It could be extremely hard to be seen and heard, however I lean into my strength as The Queen of Business Organisation. This is the beginning of what makes me different. A business coach can cover many things, as I do: marketing, social media, launching and of course, branding.

The best practice for you and your business is to lean into your strengths when you position yourself. My strength is strategy, systems, and automation, which all lead to business organisation and operations. This is just the start of what sets me apart. Other mentors may teach marketing, but do they have a simple way for you to plan it, refer back to it and manage your marketing going forward? That's what I do. I create these systems and simple strategies to make business less overwhelming.

All of this is what makes my USP true. The ability to be organised and implement strategies, regardless of my circumstances shows my true uniqueness as a business mentor, because let's face it, 90% of the human population give up. This statistic can be proven by the statistic that only 10% of business owners succeed. According to the Investopedia personal finance article, 90% of businesses fail, with the most common mistakes being that start-ups don't do any budgeting, go through cash too quickly, lack research, do not define a specific target market, fail to establish a business plan and hire employees too quickly. Take that 10% and look at how many of those succeed in making six figures and you have a very small percent. In the UK alone, only 2% of people earn over six figures (credit, The Times).

I came across a quote that reminds me regularly of what I need to do to reach the top 2%:

"To join the top 2%, you have to do what 98% won't."

This is why my message is to help others achieve more income with an online service-based business, because I have achieved it by doing what I do.

Think about what makes you, you and what you do differently. Often, it's a personal strength that you bring into your business. You are your USP. You just have to discover it and lead with it.

The most damaging thing in my career has been a niche

shift. There are always going to be challenges with every shift you make. In 2023 I had already spent previous years learning all the business skills (tried and tested), money management and mindset, left my employed job, I even stopped running networking events and was left with one focus, this business. The alignment wasn't still fully there. I was marketing as a creative business coach and realised that actually I loved working with clients in holistic industries and the impact it had when their services succeeded. My focus on business organisation had become stronger and I had become clear on who I was, more a mentor than a coach. In the midst of a huge house move after my husband's knee replacement surgery, juggling boxes holding our lives possessions and struggling with managing home and business whilst he was off his feet, I decided to come away from coaching creatives completely. I had already pre-warned clients and shifted slowly over months leading up to this point, but I was holding on through fear and naturally I began losing clients and realised it was a direct result of my heart and passion not being in what I was doing.

The Visual Brand Organisation

At this point in the journey, I am sharing with you, it's appropriate to share the evolution of the re-brand from creative business coach to *The Queen of Business Organisation*. I brightened up my brand colours, I worked more on my USP, and I announced the change to my clients, then publicly.

At the time it felt like they all disappeared overnight, but in reality, the shift in messaging meant that over a period of months, during one of the most challenging times of my life, they left my membership, didn't continue with one-to-one work and slowly but surely my income depleted. At the time I wasn't strong enough or doing the mindset work I needed, and I didn't have a coach or mentor myself. I still don't regret any decisions I made at that point, as it led me to where I am now. They say when you're at rock bottom there is only one way you can go, and I was definitely there. I had four clients and an empty membership, which I closed. The clients I had there were paying me but not showing up and it wasn't aligned to be taking their money and sat on a zoom call waiting for someone to show up. It was another income hit but it allowed me space and time to really work on the message I needed to share. *The Queen of Business Organisation* was truly born at that point. I did what I do best, and I organised my brand, my message, and my marketing.

Looking back, I remember the awful pale blue and pink that didn't really complement each other, on the blurry graphics from a free app with limited images on my mobile that I compiled together and made a logo with. This image was terrible quality and when printed was distorted and made me feel unprofessional.

You can procrastinate on branding but it's also something that I believe you should dedicate some time to and really think about what you want. I see business owners do this part lightly all the time, myself included when I started any business I've tried and tested over the years. At first it was my keepsakes business, then I dipped my toe into network marketing with perfumes, followed by a personalised clothing boutique and then finally my business mentoring gig. The shiny objects and many ideas can often be a distraction so to start with you need to think about what you really want to do and what you love. I like perfume but it doesn't light me up with passion. I loved the idea of personalised clothes and the design ideas I had but I hated making them! The keepsakes were something I loved, and I believe that's partly why I was successful with it, but it became quite stressful over time, until I let it go.

It's not to say that mentoring and coaching is easy, as sometimes it presents its challenges, but I absolutely love it and, in my heart, I love helping others. I've always been the listening ear; the friend people trust and tell secrets to and over time as I became an adult, I found myself organising things in one way or another. I know now that my organisation skills are a result of the complete chaos I've physically been surrounded by and then the chaos in my head from my teenage years. Thankfully, as I write this, after turning thirty, I'm in a much better place now, physically, and mentally.

Why is this important? All these things have an impact, and you need to take on board your strengths and weaknesses as your personal power to stand out and brand yourself to stand out as the one you go to in your desired industry, which I truly hope is the thing you're most passionate about. First, make sure the work that you do makes you want to jump out of bed in the morning.

I can teach you about colours, fonts, shapes and symbols and their contributions to your brand, but you already know that stuff, it's basic level. What I do want to teach you though is to organise it into a brand guidelines kit. Doing this for the first time made all the difference.

- Choose your colours, 3-5 and stick with them.
- Choose your fonts, 3-5 and ensure they're readable.
- Choose your shapes, images, symbols that represent your business.

Then add them to a brand kit on Canva or create a sheet that you can look at if you need to. I remember at first printing mine out and pinning it on my wall above my desk so that my brand was front of mind in everything I do, and it doesn't just come to the visuals, it's about words too.

Content makes up a huge chunk of what you do as an online marketer. There are so many words that have an impact upon. Think about your title, who you are. Think about your values as a brand and as a person. Think about your tagline. Think about your brand statement. All these words have an impact on how you present yourself in the online world but also face to face when you meet people. My suggestion is that you create a brand guidelines document, and, in this document, you answer those basic questions but always refer to and use them in everything that you do. This allows your true brand to never be lost but it's also okay for these to change over time.

Your brand document:

- Who are you? What do you do?
- Who do you help? Specifically.
- What are your values?
- What's your superpower? Your unique selling point? Why are you the one to choose?
- What's your tagline?
- What's your brand statement?
- What's your brand story? Compact into five key points.
- What impact do you have? How do you transform your clients' lives? What problems do you solve?
- How do you solve those problems?
- Why are you passionate about doing this? What is your reason why?
- What's in the future for your brand? Where do you want to take your business? Where do you want to take your clients?

Create your document and keep it safe. Refer to it when creating content, planning new business ideas or you need to reconnect with your purpose.

Your Message, your Story, and your Pillars

As my journey continued, I found myself at another pivotal point. My house move was complete. Husband's surgery done. Huge brand shift done. What next? Well, I poured all my energy into creating a mastermind that I was excited about under a new brand name and niche. *Sustainable Sales: The Mastermind* was created, and I was fuelled with fire once again. I was directing my messaging at holistic service-based business owners, believing I was finally where I needed to be. I launched this service I was fully behind and excited to get started with, only to sell no places. Not one single space. Still holding on with my four clients, one of my friends asked me, “What are you going to do now?” I made the decision there and then in Summer 2023 that I was going to do it again. I was so sure that this was the one. I had a vision and felt empowered to ensure my work wasn’t wasted. I did exactly as I said I would and continued the work on building an audience under this brand identity and in September 2023 I welcomed my first four clients into my mastermind, all fully aligned with my new direction.

Every question in the brand organisation section contributes to your overall brand message. This is particularly important if you are to remain consistent across your marketing. Remember this, as it will change the trajectory of your business. I want you to remember a quote I once heard that really struck a realisation with me and impacted my results.

‘A confused mind always says no.’

In reality if you don’t have a consistent message then you are going to confuse anyone that's in your audience or network. They cannot buy if they don't understand who you are, what you do and how you help them. A clear, confident message is so important.

Look back on your answers to the previous questions, these will help you be clear in exactly what your message is, so that you can go and share it with the world.

As part of your branding document, I mentioned your story and that's for good reason: you need to communicate how you came to be where you are right now and why you are the go-to for your service over anybody else.

Part of your story should be your lived, unique experience because nobody else can duplicate that, because it's unique to you. Very much like my own family dynamic or managing life with a husband with disabilities, health issues and regular surgeries, whilst my SEN child refuses school and has daily meltdowns and exclusions. Juggling these things with my own mental health battles, two other children and a dog. In the thick of it, we also decluttered our life and threw in a house move! That's my story but what's truly unique about it is that I still managed to create a successful, thriving business. That is my unique selling point, overcoming adversity and succeeding in extraordinary circumstances. The story behind it is *how* I manage to do this, which impacts the people I help. It's through business organisation and focused business management that my successful sold-out programmes, increase in clients and high recurring income became possible.

That's my story and it's important to note that this is why I'm shit hot at what I do, because nobody organises like I do. I've never seen anyone categorise their website pages, create systems for tracking everything and managing the finer details that make a huge impact. I'm a productive planner and big action taker and this shines through in my story. So be super clear on what your story is and lead with your power, your experiences, and your credentials too, if you want to throw those in. Sometimes this takes time to find, takes work to discover and takes trial and error to see what your strengths are. When you discover your strengths, lean into those, and let them be the unique part of you that shines through. Self-motivation is easier to discover that way, which will spur you on to take the necessary action, however I often hear that my peers in the business community can do the plan, learn the things but the biggest block is following through with self-motivation and taking action. This is where it's important to endure you have clarity on why you are doing this. Why do you want to run this business? Why do you want to sell your services? Going back to those values as a brand and connecting with those daily to offer the motivation you need, with clarity around the goals that you want to achieve.

Which leads me to your pillars, these are 'themes' that your brand has. I recommend five of them and these are what you mostly talk about within your marketing. You want the services you offer to relate to them, but also the value that you give, in which you help people, to relate too.

Decide what exactly it is that you are going to talk about and become known for. Add these to your brand document too, to return to.

For example, my brand pillars are:

- Business Strategy
- Time, productivity
- Freedom & balance
- Profit, money & sales
- Planning & business Organisation

If you know me at all, you will know that these topics fit me perfectly.
Now I want you to decide on yours.

Marketing Master

Now that you feel you have built the foundations of your brand, you should be ready to start marketing. Now here is where one key thing makes a difference, that I know many first-time business owners trip up.

You need a plan. Winging it may work, but it's only going to take you so far and unless you're an organised, efficient, and confident leader, you're probably going to get overwhelmed very fast and burn out. This book was designed to avoid exactly that. So, I want you to know is that planning needs to become part of your normal. It's non-negotiable.

One thing I wish I had done in the very beginning, was sit down and spend time on building a bulk of content from my pillars, as it would have saved so much stress in future and help overcome content block. If content block is something you regularly face, then I'm about to share with you a method that will eliminate that.

Take those content pillars you decided, then under each one I want you to create this list:

- Quotations
- Affirmations
- Stories
- Questions
- Tips/value
- Statistics/facts
- Fun (meme/jokes)

Then finally, once you know your service suite:

- Services
- Testimonials
- Case study/transformations

What this does is make marketing EASY! Now you can create all the types of content around that one content pillar, save it and never run out of content again. The initial creation will take some time, but then once you have got a batch of content, you're good for having something ready when you struggle with content block and knowing what to post.

When you are marketing a particular service, I recommend to always share content related to that service, e.g. If I'm selling my planner, I will share quotations, affirmation, and tips around planning. My overall focus is on that one thing, making it easy for my audience to know what action to take.

You also want to always dive into your brand message, story, and clients' stories alongside your regular content, to create awareness of what you do and really cement yourself as the go- to expert, to create authority.

Now remember I like to be organised, so I created Canva folders for my themed content, created a doc for all my quotations, another for my affirmations etc. and added them to my relevant folder, so that they're easy to find. There's nothing worse than hunting for a particular graphic you'd like to share but wasting time because you don't know where it is. In fact, organisation saves you so much time, which means you can do more, get more results and have more, whilst helping more people. That's the dream for me, true balance, and less chaos.

Once I had nailed the above, the branding, the message and begun using within my marketing I felt finally in control of the direction I needed to be, with a clear vision of what's possible. There is no coincidence that in winter of 2023 I created my first signature programme and sold out of all spaces I had available. In a matter of months, I went from four clients, to over twenty! I had three strong services available, bringing in more money and stacking my income. I could see the impact that practising what I preach, and being aligned with my product suite and branding was having.

Once everything was aligned, the results were coming and

more than ever before, in a way I could manage. It was at that point I began facing the debt too. More income meant that I could pay it off and so I set a goal to have it all paid within eight months. Flash forward to now and I only have £700 debt remaining and it is going down consistently each month. There are no coincidences. Consistency with this new brand message and going all in on marketing was working.

Chapter 5

Calling in the Clients

Character Clarity

Selling to your ideal clients is like writing a story, you need to know the characters as though they are real, living people where you describe them like you can see them in front of you. It's the same with your business and the person you are aiming to sell to. Our thoughts around sales tends to go towards the negative experiences you have had from being sold to like cold callers, car deals or being stopped in the street. None of those methods we like or enjoy, and it paves the way for the narrative that selling is bad. Selling is serving someone what they need. In your mind's eye, picture serving your ideal clients with what they need. It's much better when you tap into the idea of helping someone rather than just selling to them.

Hopefully you will feel more comfortable with selling to this person, once you reframe that that you know you're helping them. The system I have created for connecting to your ideal client is creating a 'Dreamy Client's Brief' or what most marketers call an avatar. You can physically draw or design what this person looks like but the document I create is all about connecting with who they are, what problems they have and the results they're looking for. I create a document to cement the idea and become a reference every time I'm creating social media content, writing copy for sales pages, or going live and talking to my audience. You may want to update this over time too, as you and your business develops and evolves.

Getting clarity on WHO you are serving is very stereotypical. It's probably the only time it is okay to be stereotypical. The biggest mistake with deciding who you are selling to is thinking about who *could* buy, rather than who *would* buy. Remember, 'a confused mind says no.' The proof is in my own story and how going from being a creative business owner and becoming a creative business coach, targeting creative business owners I succeeded and landed clients on day one, then changing my niche and getting specific and instead messaging to women in service-based businesses. When I became *The Queen of Business Organisation*, I was speaking to just 'business owners' and as soon as I narrowed down and targeted 'service-based businesses' I attracted more clients. One of the reasons I have been able to sell out programs and sign new clients consistently is because of how targeted both my ideal clients were. There are no coincidences (again!) that once I narrowed down who I was selling to, my business grew.

It's about knowing the demographics: gender, age, location, income/occupation but also knowing the psychographics: personality, lifestyle, attitudes, social status, activities, interests, and opinions. You really must know your dream client and what makes them the one who would buy what you have to offer. Think about their common struggles and their core desires.

For example, my dreamy client struggles with selling, it's because she has no strategy in place (most of the things in this book). She isn't clear enough on her vision, values and message and needs to get organised with her daily business activities because she desires more freedom, through earning more. She wants to book the dream holiday, treat the kids over summer and not have to count the pennies on her next shopping trip. She isn't looking for a millionaire lifestyle, but she is looking to improve her life day by day. Does this sound like you? If you resonate then I have clearly nailed my ideal client persona. I know her so well because she is me. She is the version of me who has been through the journey I am sharing with you in this book.

I'm not touching on sales just yet, but I want to share with you the secret to buying behaviour, because once you fully understand this, alongside clarity on your ideal client, you can implement it into your marketing and your sales will increase easily. It's simply because once you know and communicate this in your content, you attract the right people, because the message hits.

People buy either for wealth, health, or relationships.

What you sell will fall into these categories. For example, I sell services that help clients earn more money and create more freedom, which fits into wealth, but it has a direct impact on their health and relationships too. Noticing the connection in what you sell can effectively help you present the transformation that you can offer your client. When people buy, there are typical 'triggers' that their buying behaviour is a direct result of.

Buying behaviour triggers:

- Earn money.
- Save money.
- Elevate Status.
- Get out of pain.

It is easy to see how what I do impacts a client's buying behaviours. I help them earn money and get out of pain, because the stress of needing more money is eased, the overwhelm of not knowing how to grow their business is eased as I teach them how. Often there may be one or more buying triggers. I want to share another example to help you recognise your clients' triggers. When I was selling memory keepsakes, my ideal client was buying to elevate status and get out of pain. My clients often purchased because they unfortunately suffered a bereavement and when buying from me it was for themself, to get out of pain with grief and create something to capture a beautiful memory, but they were often purchased as gifts and I recognised that they were quite proud of this gift, as it is unique, more thoughtful, and quite expensive too. I imagined my ideal client revealing this to family and how they may feel. I know how I would feel, like my gift was the best! This elevated the status of being granted the best gift giver. Nobody can beat something like that. People always want to be liked and feel good enough, which is what the desire is for this client in buying this gift.

Think about your ideal client and how buying from you moved them from pain to pleasure. This is where you can connect with them on a whole new level.

It may be clear now why I had to change who I was speaking to and why I had to 'break up' with my existing creative clients, to be able to move into this new target market and niche. Marketing to just anyone is simply going to mean that what you say or do isn't going to be attractive to anyone. It was a tough call for me, but when I could tap into my new client's desire of helping others with their services whilst creating freedom for themselves, it just secured the sale even easier, and the consistent welcome of new clients continued from the moment I had relaunched my mastermind and sold out my group programme.

Lead Generation Organisation

You're set on who your ideal client is, you've started talking to them with your content, now what? You want to get those enquiries in and generate leads!

A lead is a person who is interested in what you have to

offer. At this point you want to ensure you track who is asking questions, why they're asking and where they asked it. These days we use many platforms to communicate our message and so it can easily be a lot to remember. This is why having a lead tracking system is important.

In my first business I would get phone calls, emails, messages on my personal Facebook profile, messages on my business page, comments on my posts and occasionally Instagram. All these avenues I had built for people to see what I offer were great, but a lead could easily get lost in the transaction as I posted more content, received more messages, and lost track of who was contacting me, what they wanted and where they had reached out. At that moment in time, I began taking note of the name, the enquiry, where they enquired and scheduled a reminder to follow up days later. I used my Google calendar for this and ensured that every time a potential customer asked a question, I made a note of it. These days, it's easy for the client to get lost in all my other tasks on my calendar, so I created a system to track them separately to my to-do list, using Trello. Trello is free and I love it! You can use something else, a notebook, a spreadsheet, or notes on your mobile, it doesn't matter as long as you know who you're intending to talk to, what their needs are and how to contact them.

Here's what I track:

- Their initial enquiry: this puts them on my lead board.
- Point of contact/follow up after initial enquiry.
- Their reply.

- If I have invited them to a free zoom clarity call and sent the link.
- If they have booked a call.
- Follow up after the call straight away and propose an offer.
- Follow up two days after the call.
- Won: they enrolled as a client.
- Lost: they didn't enrol as a client.

It's a lot to track, isn't it? Your lead flow will depend on the steps you want to take for your business, however that is how I manage mine. That is why I set up a Trello board for easy management, plus it is why I am *The Queen of Business Organisation*, I really do organise everything as much as I can within my business!

The idea is that the lead starts at the first list (on my lead Trello board) and moves through to either be won or lost. Some people may sit in the middle for a while, which is why it's important to take note of their name and needs, so that I can connect with them regularly.

I must admit, this prospecting did make me feel the icky and created a bad sales narrative at first, because it felt like I was treating people like numbers or money makers. The thing is, I knew I couldn't help anyone if I couldn't remember what their needs were. As my audience grew, I was dealing with thousands following my social media pages and hundreds on my email list, so I needed a way to capture those who were coming forward to take my focus and attention. It also became easier once I realised that I don't do the hard sell and I connect with people and treat them like people and not a meal ticket, so it was easy to get over and increased my chances of getting a result.

This is your reminder that it's okay to do this work when selling. You're a business owner now and it's time to step into that CEO role. It actually services people better if you can remember their name, their interests, and their needs as your potential clients.

As well as having your set up to track leads, you have to take action to attract them. I often see business owners do this only when launching something new, but the reality is that you should be prioritising lead generation all the time and not just now and again. This will grow your following, build your audience and lead to more sales. It's the first thing that you should do as a non-negotiable daily income producing activity.

Again, there is no coincidence that when I was consistently ensuring I connected with more people and welcomed them into my world that my sales increased. If you have your message right, you have to position it in front of the right people. Know who you serve and go out and find them.

At this point in my story, I had signed more clients than I had ever had and with my programmes I was offering bonuses that they could access too. I was glad for being organised, because client management could very quickly become overwhelming if I wasn't!

Onboarding and Retention

Once I had successfully relaunched my mastermind and sold out my first big group programme, I had over twenty clients, so I needed to streamline as much as possible, ensuring everything was easy for me and my clients.

I noticed a gap in the market, nobody seemed to focus on what to do once you sign the clients! Of course, deliver a great service, but what about onboarding them into your service? What about the next steps? What about streamlining this process to make it super simple?

I'm going to share something with you that I have only shared with my business besties and mastermind clients, as I was figuring out if this process could work. My Onboarding automation process.

I have already shown you the system I have to generate the lead and now I'm taking you beyond, where the client says yes! Well, this stage starts at the point that they book a call. My system takes it from there, however I do like to personalise and connect, by following up, but here's what happens in the background:

1. Welcome email: client is welcomed and provided with contract for the service.
2. Client is introduced to the features of the service e.g. Learning portal or support group.
3. Client is welcomed to the group community (if there is one).

4. Follow up reminder to complete any steps, e.g. Sign contract or join community.
5. Dates for diary and reminder emails when live calls are happening.

This may look confusing or overwhelming at first but remember to take one step at a time and this can be automated to save time. Realistically, doing these individual steps manually per client could burn you out, whilst managing other aspects of your business, which is why I'm hugely FOR business automation as early as possible. Imagine doing all the contracts, the payment links, the welcome emails, and orientations etc. individually with nearly thirty clients (which I have at the time of writing this book). I would spend more time back and forth ironing out all the wrinkles, rather than supporting clients with what they really need or working further on my business. This is why I am a huge advocate for systems and processes, because it does make everything easier and smoother. You set out as you mean to go on, so if you are reading this with only one client or handful, just know that if you aim to increase your client base and increase your income, you must make space for it.

I remember listening to a podcast by Denise Duffield-Thomas, where she stated that if you want to manifest more one to one clients but haven't created space for them in your diary then that's blocking them from coming to you, because the universe cannot find space for them. It is the same with the systems you have in place to onboard clients, if you are not prepared to manage them, they will not come in. It does involve working with tech and I know in the beginning it can be scary, hard, and confusing and I have been exactly where you are, but I overcame it, so you can too.

Remember, as we navigated through earlier in this book, you can learn the skills, you can figure out the 'how,' you only need to choose to have the mindset for it. This is a book, so there's only so much I can write to support this but do know that you can reach me at any time @queenofbusinessorganisation if you have any questions in relation to this. I help my clients with processes to streamline and save time like this all the time!

You've done the whole journey, the leading, the onboarding, what next? Yes, there's a next step! It's much easier to retain a client than it is to sell to a new one, especially if you're delivering a great service! That's exactly what needs to be part of your strategy with your existing clients.

The first place to start is that service suite you mapped out. Each service needs to fill a gap with where your client is on their journey and it's important to ensure you can lead from one place to the next. Once your clients work with you comes to an end, always offer a next step. They won't automatically ask to stay working with you unless they know how they can! I recommend sending them a recommendation of the next step for them before your current commitment ends and allow them to prepare for it. Not only does this retain clients and income for you, but it also ensures that your client isn't going to then find it challenging to continue without your support and end up back at the beginning with the problem they came to you with. Of course, the work you have done would have moved them along but there's a lot of power in accountability.

Always be mindful of the next step.

Master the Management

Yes, there's still more to master around the management of bringing in clients and knowing where you're at with them. At this point I'm counting on you having multiple clients working with you, in different ways. This is where you could easily forget what you've committed to, for example who had a bonus 121 sessions to take. This is where having a client management system in place will do the work.

When I implemented this, it was all about simplicity and having everything in one simple place, plus I love a spreadsheet! Feeling overwhelmed with what I had promised and who to, I needed to do something to manage my relationships and services with clients better. Here is what I did.

First of all, write down every service you currently offer, from the top tier 121 work, right down to group work, memberships etc.

For me, it looked like this:

- 121 Mentoring.
- Sustainable Sales 6-month mastermind.
- Foundations 12-month programme.
- Organisation Implementation 12-week mini mastermind.
- Sales Success System course.
- Passive classes/bundles etc.

Once I had mapped out the service I was currently offering, I could then list underneath each service, the clients I had in and their monthly instalments.

121 Mentoring:

- Client 1 £150
- Client 2 £150
- Client 3 £150

Mastermind

- Client 4 £333
- Client 5 £167
- Client 6 £333
- Client 7 £167

...and so on. Then I could add up the projected payments for each month and be aware of the money coming in, who had a payment plan, what the monthly instalments were and when they ended. This way, it becomes easy to spot any missed payments and I could make note of when payments or their contract comes to an end to ensure I offer the options for them to continue to work with me or fill that new income gap in my financial spreadsheet.

The truth is, I REALLY hate numbers. They get mixed up in my head and fry my brain, but they are very important in business and so I am a huge advocate of knowing your numbers and managing your finances. I know it's not easy at all, which is why I love keeping things super simple and I created a client management sheet, which allows me to track all their recurring payments. I have added a copy of the document to your bonus resources section that goes along with this book, you can find it within my Organised Business toolkit. Scan the QR code at the end of the book to access it and start tracking payments and managing your clients in an efficient way. You're welcome!

I really feel truly grateful that I set all of this up *before* I then sold out my mini mastermind this year (2024), because I would have otherwise been overwhelmed managing nearly thirty clients, with all their different payment plans, services, and bonuses. Let this be the sign that you need to be organised as you grow your business, otherwise it can become overwhelming with more to manage as you grow.

Chapter 6

Media Mastery

The Platform, the Foundations

Now that we are halfway through this book, we are really setting those foundations for you to start, grow and scale your business and I am so excited to see the outcome you have. Please tag and **share on social media @queenofbusinessorganisation** anything that you implement and learn or get a result from.

Social media has played a huge part in my business growth, when I was first getting into the world of business, things were just starting out with social media and marketing. It may be hard to believe now, but most online social platforms weren't as popular as they are now, with everyone using them. Facebook isn't that old itself, at the time of me writing this book, in 2024. These platforms became big overnight and grew and grew, with everyone rushing to get onto them and connect with each other, which then businesses noticed had an opportunity for them, me included.

I was playing with social media before I had ever thought about running a business. As a first-time mum, used to working from age sixteen and on maternity leave with a baby that actually slept well, fed well and was very good. Once we were both fed, whilst my husband was at work, I was bored. So, I began an online mum community, mostly for new mums like me, especially as I had moved to the other side of Leeds, I had no friends or family around, other than my in-laws, who were still quite new to me at the time. I wanted to connect with others like me and I had no idea what I was doing, it was very much a learn on the go scenario, but it took off.

Within three months I had an admin team and we reached 8000+ followers on our Facebook page. Within six months, I was hosting giveaways and being sponsored by small businesses who were looking for visibility. I loved it and realised I was onto something. I was already exploring new creative hobbies, creating soft furnishing with needle and thread and thinking about what I could sell. I had easily tapped into this online world and had more interesting ideas and one I rolled with.

Fast forward eleven years later and I would never have expected that I would be teaching you how to start a business using social media and other marketing and business strategies. Yet here I am! I wouldn't have believed anyone if they told me that I would be choosing my work hours, teaching others and be well known across the UK as

The Queen of Business Organisation. All of this began because of social media. Playing with a few platforms and seeing what I could do with it. These days I know much better though. I know not to join in the like for like and comment for comment threads. To be blunt, they are a waste of time and don't work! I have had many argue against my opinion over the years and I could explain all day why they don't work but instead, just like I'm saving you time by telling you not to partake in those types of 'networking' I would rather save you time by telling you how to plan to use social media to have an impact on your business in a positive way.

Okay, so let's begin with some basics. The first rules of social media management are.

1. Don't put all your eggs into one basket.
2. Don't overwhelm yourself with too many platforms.

A bit contradictory, isn't it? Both are true though.

You don't own social media, so you really don't want to rely on only that. This is where email marketing comes in, which I highly recommend you learn and implement within your business (and I can help with that!) These days, in this ever-growing world of new social platforms launching and evolving all the time (think Clubhouse, Twitter becoming X and Meta/Instagram introducing Threads) you need to be visible everywhere and create as many points of contact as possible, you want people to see you as much as possible.

At the same time, if you try to be everywhere it can be overwhelming and very quickly lead to burnout. Managing content and engagement on many platforms can be tough without a workforce behind you. So, what do you do? My advice is to begin with two social media platforms and an email list as a starter, then introduce more over time when you are ready.
Choose your platforms wisely. It has to be somewhere you enjoy hanging out and your ideal client will be using too. I personally favour Facebook and Instagram! I don't understand Twitter and I never joined Clubhouse. A reminder that you also don't have to join in on something just because everyone else is. We are grown-ups now; we don't have to give into peer pressure. You do you and you will get the best out of any platform you are using.

Now you have chosen where, now what? I have some basic foundations that can be applied to most social media platforms.

Display picture - A photo of you if you are an individual or personal brand, not your cat or dog, your kids, or a random waterfall. They are all beautiful, but people buy from people. Keep your image updated too. Changed your hair? Update your display picture.

Cover image - A great space to utilise. Yeah, it would be nice to share a family holiday picture, but if you are using social media for business, unless that holiday pic is relevant then isn't it best to use this space to capture attention? A cover image is a great space to add a call to action, give your viewer an option of a next step to take with you.

Bio - Keeps it simple. Use language that your ideal client will understand, something that a 7-year-old would understand. Telling the world, the long-worded degree you have that nobody has heard of is not going to help your business. Save that to explain later. Simply state what you do, who for and the result you get.

Link - If there is a space for a link, use it. You want to be clever with this though. Don’t add a link tree link, which then lists one thousand different options. Keep it simple. One link, with one or two calls to actions. My go- to is always, one way to be part of my audience even further e.g. another social media platform, one way to join my email list e.g. with a freebie and finally a way to buy from me e.g. a current offer. Don't over complicate it. A confused mind always says no, and you want a potential client to act.

Highlights/Featured - These sections are available on most platforms now and are a great opportunity to capture attention. I would recommend featuring the same three things as you do within your link and direct to your link or add a link to the post if you can. Another way to join your audience, get onto your email list or buy from you right now?

Take some time to audit your own social media.

Ask yourself, is it clear what it is that you do? Then really see if it is clear *who* you do it for. Remember when I guided you through speaking to your target market? This is where that work comes into play. That work is the most vital for lead generation, yet I see so many businesses miss including it anywhere they show up. You definitely want to be sure that your social media is attracting the right people.

Is it easy to take the next step with you? What I mean by asking this, is can I go onto your profile and either get onto your email list or buy from you? You want to make it as easy as possible.

Finally, a top tip. Don't just sling your website or shop link everywhere. I get it, you want more sales but even if someone does click, it's a wasted click, as people are not going to warm enough to buy unless you have warmed them up. Your social media platforms should direct to another way to connect further with you by consuming more content. For example, the link in your bios should either lead to a social community, e.g. your Facebook group or go to your email list opt in. This way you capture them, instead of sending them to a shop where you could lose them. Don't worry about wanting to sell to them, you can do that later in your social media posts and emails. Social media platforms are great at being used to funnel people into your world.

When I rebranded and became The Queen of Business Organisation, I had a lot of work to do! I overhauled all my social media and updated all my images, links, and descriptions in my bios. I am always changing it and tweaking it regularly too, to ensure the message is aligned with where I am at currently and how I want to communicate with my ideal clients. At this point, after revealing the big change in what I was doing with my focus for the business, I also upgraded everything else. My free opt-ins evolved when I added more value, and I had a professional copywriter do the copy for my pages and email sequences. It pays off to use an expert!

The myths the truth and the choice

I have been really looking forward to this section. It's a chance to really educate on what's what and how you should grow your business, and the truth is, the way you want to!

We all know that engagement is important on social media because the more people engage the more your post is pushed out to more people, and this is on any platform. It's just how algorithms work, no matter how many times they are updated.

But let's bust some myths:

- Adding engaging questions, like what's your favourite ice cream, will help you.

No. It won't. This will attract everyone and not help your business grow at all. Targeted posts and engaging questions are much better.

- Comment swaps/comment for comment and like for like threads will increase reach.

True but they won't get you sales and will waste time. It's nice to support each other but when you have to leave fifty comments on posts you aren't interested in every day, it's boring and it's not income producing. Focus on income producing activities instead. Plus, if the fifty others commenting are not your ideal client, they are not going to buy and the algorithm thinks they like your posts, so it pushes it out to more people like them, which increases your reach, but to the wrong people, lessening you reaching ideal clients and getting a sale. It does more harm than good.

- You must post x number of times per day.

Nope. You should only post as much as you want to. If a 'social guru' tells you to post three times per day then that can very quickly become overwhelming, so you rush posts, burn out and end up not posting for weeks then kick yourself, start again and create an awful cycle. Quality over quantity. Of course, the more you post the more visible you are but start with one post per day and build up over time. Consistency over being constant is more important.

- You must post at x time of day to be seen.

This one is just very unrealistic. If the guru is telling me, I have to be available to post at 4pm every day then that's not going to happen. I finish work at 3pm on a typical day.

I am not going to be sticking around to post live. Scheduling for the win. It is better for you to schedule and post, than have nothing posted because you intend to post at 4pm, you were busy and got distracted then beat yourself up because you forgot to post. Done is better than perfect in all scenarios and we cannot completely control the algorithm anyway.

- You must engage twenty minutes before you post and twenty minutes after.

Ok, let's crunch some numbers. If you stick by this method, then you post three times a day, that's a whopping two hours per day! That is not including content creation or serving clients and the many other jobs you need to do to run your business. This is not a sustainable strategy. I know that posting and ghosting isn't a good idea either, however you can come and check your notifications and respond to comments when you're available and people have cottoned onto the engagement strategies and that you are only liking their post to get likes back. Instead, engage with those you genuinely want to engage with. If you really want to engage to grow, look for others in your industry or similar industry and engage with them. This will be far less time consuming, enjoyable and will get you seen by the right people. Or put those two hours into collaborations and generate new leads to your social media instead.

The truth is, there is no one quick fix to grow your business on social media. The platforms update and change all the time, you just have to be savvy and keep an eye on it. The biggest thing that will make a difference is consistency and learning your platform of choice like the back of your hand.

The choice. You have a choice every day to waste time on these strategies that will burn you out or you can take my advice and find an easier way. In all honesty if your brand message communicates effectively then you won't need to waste time because the algorithm and your consistency will work for you.

Final thought on this, do you think those big-time coaches earning millions are spending two hours per day engaging on social media, worrying about how often to post and what time of day to post? I don't think so! Take it from someone who used to worry about all of this and got zero results. When I got strategic instead, I was able to start earning four figures consistently, per month. It's not millions but it has been enough to achieve some of my biggest goals and I want to inspire you to make the right choices for you when it comes to organising how you are going to manage your business using social media. Plus, now I get the fun of aiming to work towards a six-figure career, doing what I love! I look forward to that!

I used to follow all the above 'rules' that I have shared with you. One day I decided it wasn't working for me and I adapted. The best thing I ever did was build my business my way. That's not to say that you shouldn't take advice from some of the social media marketers out there but be mindful of how time consuming these actions can be and impact you mentally. Stick with me though, for real and raw strategy work. I didn't learn any of this by accident, it was absolutely by doing all the things in the way that didn't work and the lack of results it got, so that I could be here today busting myths for you. If I can earn a consistent income doing things 'my way' and binning off the generic advice, which let's face it, has come about via Chinese whispers online, well you can do it too!

The Elements & The Power of Planning

You didn't think that *The Queen of Business Organisation* was going to let you get away with no planning of your social media, did you?

I really enjoy this part! I do this every single month with some of my clients, and it helps us get really focused on how we are being intentional with social media and content marketing each month.

You may have gathered by now that I enjoy creating processes to manage business easier. I am all about simplicity and love a checklist or method to get things done quicker. That is exactly what I have in place every month when I map out my strategy. Note I do plan more than social media, my monthly strategy also includes:

- Email marketing
- Podcast episodes
- YouTube videos
- Networking

- Collaborations
- Blogging

I do a lot, but I have a team to support me. I think about all of these and social media first and how I am using them all to sell what I have to offer, then I add value too!

The platforms we use these days have a wide range of variety and so you can do so much with them to increase your visibility, and you really want to capitalise on this. I am going to use one platform as an example to explain how to plan how you use your platform and opportunities as much as you possibly can.

Facebook. This platform allows me to create a profile, a business page, and a group. These are the main elements there.

Each element can be broken down even further:

Profile:

- Posts
- Live
- Reels
- Stories
- Post into other groups
- Engage on feed posts
- Create events
- Add friends
- Highlights
- Pinned post

Business page:

- Posts
- Lives
- Events
- Reels
- Pinned post

Group:

- Posts
- Live
- Reels
- Polls
- Events
- Guides
- Featured section

Right there on one platform is a list of so many elements that you can use to grow your business. Start with this list and plan out what you are going to use, when and where. Remember you don't have to use them all daily, keep it simple. Starting with a plan is the first step in preparation to act and achieve your goals.

I urge you to copy this list and use it, expand on it.

Planning is so powerful. Without sitting down and making decisions on what I am doing, how I am doing it and when I am doing it, I would just aimlessly sail through each day without intentions and aligned actions that would produce income. I have a term for people who don't have a plan, they are the 'Wing-it-Wendy's' of the world! It's okay though, with the help of this book, step-by-step you can become a 'Sorted Sandra.'

I have a 'Sort Your Strategy Quiz' that will tell you which entrepreneurial avatar you are, a 'Wing-it-Wendy,' 'Sorted Sandra,' or 'Level Up Lana.' At the time of writing this book only two people have ever achieved Lana status, and most people are Wendy. Take the quiz and see what result you get! You also get a free strategy guide. (Available via the QR at the back of this book.)

I am so passionate about planning, because in the last three years it has served me so well with my business growth. I have already shared my story with you, the ups and downs and how I went from burning my business to the ground and rising from the ashes. When I transformed from those four clients to selling out multiple offers, what happened next amazed me even more. I got focused more on planning and being very strategic, which as a result lead to increased visibility, mostly using social media and by the start of 2024 I signed a client contract that paid me £2k per month, then I hit £5k earning in one month and the best part was, I was only working four days per week!

At this point I really did feel unstoppable. A belief was born like it never had been before because I began to realise what I was great at and capable of. I showcased this through my social media content, and it attracted more clients to me. I wanted to bottle up this feeling, so that everyone could experience it. At that time, I saw an opportunity to overcome the previous stress I had faced around the money management and debt I had obtained, and I got a handle on my finances and started paying off the debt that I owed. I do want to state that it didn't go as far as having the ability to affect my family, but it was really stressful when an actual letter arrived in the post, stating I had failed to meet any payments. That was the final straw for me and nudged me to face up to how I had been spending and get it all sorted out.

Social Success the Practical Steps

In my opinion, there are three ways to achieve social success when it comes to your business.

1. Make it as simple as possible.
2. Keep on trialling, testing & learning. Social media is always changing.
3. Love what you're doing! Don't waste time doing things that don't align with you.

Let's dive a bit deeper.

The reality is, when you first begin building a business you may be committed to many other things in life that take your time. Your business will take time to build, there's no doubt about it, however you can make it easier by finding a path of least resistance.

My message from this is, take the path of least resistance. Let go of what isn't working or what you don't need right now and find a quicker, easier way. In my mind, it always starts with a system.

Content is king on social media and so it's clear you need to master it to succeed. My system for success is to batch create as much as you can, schedule or repurpose. The system I use is 'banking.' Every piece of content you create, save it and bank it for later. Bank new ideas to use in future and organise them into categories and topics to make content creation and posting easier. Getting your content out there is key for visibility.

As mentioned above, it did take quite some time for me in my first business, whereas when I launched as a mentor, I welcomed in five clients straight away. The difference here was that I already had many years' experience, had built an audience full of my ideal clients and I just put my message out there, loud, and clear. All those years before had been the trialling, the testing of what works, what doesn't and learning the next new features on social media. In this game you always have to make time to learn and to practise.

A tip: when you do give those new platform features a go, new features always perform well. They will get you more reach and visibility, this is because the creators of the platform want you to use them and test out the response to the features so the algorithm will favour it and put it in front of your audience.

I want to note that viral content is not the thing to chase. Going viral may boost your views and engagement but it's not going to really contribute to your business success. Simply put, connecting with your audience, building brand awareness, creating interest, and attracting their desire is what it's all about. All you can do is try different methods, different messages and ideas and see what works. I truly believe that research and auditing are the best forms of insight to give your business the fuel to drive toward a path of sales success.

Finally, do what aligns with you. Often, being stuck happens when you're not 100% sure or happy with what you're doing. I've been here before, and it was one of the biggest challenges I had to face but one of the best decisions I ever made and the biggest hurdle I've overcome.
I wasn't aligned with my keepsakes business anymore. As I was still juggling that and mentoring it was eating at my energy, so that I couldn't fully step into who I needed to be and trust myself to succeed.

If you're using social media in a way that doesn't feel right for you, don't. If you're being told what to do and it doesn't feel good to do, don't. If your business isn't 'the one' then it's time to find what is.

If something doesn't align, let it go. Don't hold on to what doesn't serve you.

In 2024 I went through yet another phase of this myself. There is quite a theme of 'letting go' throughout my story. First my NHS part time job, then my networking events, my keepsakes business and again, at the end of 2023 I closed down my membership, because it just wasn’t right for me or my ideal clients anymore. Think about what you can let go of right now and see what happens for you.

It wouldn't be me if I didn't include a process here to help support your content creation for social media. I use this method within Trello, but you can adapt this and bank your content anywhere that suits you.

First, decide upon 3-5 content pillars. These are the topics that your content typically covers. For example, one of mine is ‘business organisation.’

From each topic, you can then brainstorm types of content for each, quotes, questions, stories etc. Use the system as inspiration to brainstorm and bank content so that you never have to run out of ideas again!

Chapter 7

Creation: The Process, The Power & The Passive

Product, Service & Ideas

In this book, we've covered a lot so far. Now it's time to look at the creation of what you're selling and the process of generating an income from it. When deciding what you're going to sell, there's one thing that plays a huge part in your products and services succeeding and I would be surprised to hear if you have done it.

RESEARCH!

I truly believe that doing research around the ideas that you have leads to a higher chance of succeeding. This is because you can find out exactly what your target market wants and needs and create it.

The first place I recommend you start when deciding on

what you're going to sell is getting an old school pen and paper and start mind mapping. I do this every year and mind map my ideas. I then take those ideas and use some of them for my business plan for the year ahead.
I'm really structured in what I do next and organise the important elements of each service or product I'm going to offer.

- When do I plan to launch it or market and sell it?
- What is the price point?
- How many people do I want to sell to?
- How much income will that generate?

Then when it's nearer to the actual launch of the service I do research ahead of time.

In 2023, ahead of my Foundations twelve-month programme launch I did research into what my audience needed support with, looked at what my clients had needed the most and how much on average people were spending on business investments in terms of support. I then created the programme, adapted from content I already had. I created it to match up with my findings and in eight weeks I sold all my spaces on the programme plus a lot of my planning bundles.

In May 2024 I used the same method, research first, taking one of my original ideas and finding out what was needed at that moment in time. I launched my mini mastermind; Organisation Implementation and it sold out ahead of schedule before the month was out. This not only

worked well in terms of achieving one of business goals and creating a new income stream, but it also left space to create a new opportunity to earn more money and pre-sell the next round!
Concluding on the idea of research when it comes to your products or services, it's very much about knowing your target market. You really want to get to know your ideal clients.

Navigating what you are going to sell is never easy, as there are so many business models and you have some people saying you should have a launch model, some people saying you should introduce products and then experts on passive income pop up and promote that. The truth is, I decided to do it all. When navigating what products or services I wanted to sell, I simply decided to just offer both! My business runs on a launch model basis, where I open the doors to my masterminds every three months. Then in between those launches I sell some of my passive products and it feels easy to navigate. It took a long time to get to this point, because I first had to figure out who I wanted to be, what I wanted to be known for and then inject that into my services, which thankfully has happened successfully in 2024.

I decided to lean into my creativity and not wanting to focus on one thing and worth with it, rather than against it. However, I couldn't sell everything at once, so I focused on selling one service at a time and mastermind getting clients into that one service, then introduced another to keep the focus and keep it simple.

Before I wrap up this section, I know that you may be thinking, do I offer product, service, or both? I believe there's room for both and a diverse product suite has a great impact on your capacity to earn more. Ultimately though it's up to you and what you want to create, what you enjoy, and your energy can get behind and get excited about. Selling is always easy when you *feel* into it. Love it, enjoy it, be excited by it.

Coinciding Creations with Focus & Strategy

One thing that will absolutely transform your business, should you implement it, is FOCUS.
I have walked the walk myself and witnessed many aspiring entrepreneurs lacking focus with their business.

First, a plan helps with this. Secondly, changing direction too much can be a huge detriment to your consistency in all areas.

I do promote adaptation, adjust assessment before action, however if you create something new every month, build momentum and it doesn't generate results, so you stop and do something new, you're impacting your business in several ways:

1. Confusing your audience by changing just as they get clear on what you're doing. A confused mind does not buy.
2. You're burning yourself out trying to create and 'do' all the time.
3. You're breaking the flow within the business if you pivot

all the time.

Instead, I recommend deciding on offers you're sure about, something you genuinely love to sell and run with that. If it doesn't work out, break down why it didn't work. What did you do well? What didn't go well? What can you do better next time?

The key words there are ‘next time.’ If you're passionate about succeeding, there has to be a next time.

When I first launched Sustainable Sales: The Mastermind I had nobody buy my service. I launched it again and again and as I write this now my launch isn't perfect, so I keep adapting and fine tuning. I coined this idea a year ago, yet only recently have I had a huge breakthrough in what I need to do differently to succeed with it. I truly believe now that I've found the key to landing the clients I want and hitting the goals that I want. It took running the programme multiple times to get here. It took trial and error and most importantly focus. Focusing on this goal has been at the heart of this project. I could go and create something else instead. I could just face facts that a higher ticket programme isn't for me. I could do what I had done and accept neither of those as my reality. This is where I planned to focus on this four times a year to encourage the traction, I wanted to create with it. Realistically the more I continue to talk about it, *focus* on it, the more my audience warms up to the idea of it.

So how do you gain that focus? Simply just decide. Decide

right now that focus is for you and it's what you'll do. Let it be your mantra and take action.

You want to take strategic action. So, let's look at what strategy is:

1. A plan of action designed to achieve a long-term or overall aim.
2. The art of planning and directing overall military operations and movements in a war or battle.

Strategy is a mix of both for me. It's a plan of action towards my bigger goals but it's also about the specific operations and movements within my business to reach those goals.

Think about what you want to achieve.

- What actions are you taking?
- What operations do you need?
- What moves are you making?

As you implement selling your products and services, you want them to coincide with each other. Create a flow from one offer to the next. Be strategic in how you operate what you're selling and when. Thinking back to when you looked at your service suite (chapter three) and those offers co-existing with one another in terms of clients' delivery, your capacity to serve and your marketing.

Working in this way brought me to a recent part of my story, selling out my second programme in less than twelve months and increasing my recurring revenue on a consistent basis. It has been a huge achievement and so great to see. It happened because of my income becoming 'stacked' between the multiple services and products I am offering and them all generating an income.

Master the Management: Time, Money & Magic

Achieving balance is my greatest success. Money is nice, the results my clients get are amazing but ultimately the balance I have created with a life I am happy with is the one thing that I absolutely truly love, and I am in control of this. Of course, I am passionate about helping you to achieve, however that is on you, not me. I am not in control of your success, you are. Recognising this for myself and taking full responsibility, without excuses, became a huge shift within the way I behaved when it came to taking action.

Once you have read this book, I want you to be one step closer to finding your balance too, whatever that looks like for you. Whether you have a life of calm and relaxing days that just flow around your business or chaotic and busy, like mine, with kids, animals, and creative projects, it's about finding your flow in a way that works for you.

First you have to master time. You cannot take it back, you cannot create it, but what you can do is choose wisely how you spend it. Often in mentoring I discover that most business owners find time management and money management a block to progressing with business. This is where underlying issues start, because if you don't master either before you grow then once you do, it can all go tits up. I have seen many occasions of this, and I want you to succeed.

First, look at your life and business, your commitments, and responsibilities, as well as the thing you want to do too. What do you need to have included within your life? I recommend beginning with this and then deciding how much time each part of your life takes. Look at your business, decide how many hours you can commit to developing your business. It's worth being realistic and noting that in the beginning it will take more time than you like. It is about how much you really want it to succeed, whilst at the same time knowing that it isn't about working all the hours god sent and that it is about prioritising how you use your time.

The key to time management is not how much you work or how hard you work, it is instead about how efficiently you work. Working smarter and not harder is a real thing. My biggest advice for you is to always prioritise three things when you are time limited: lead generation, nurturing your audience and sales activities. Of course, you need time to implement client delivery too and all of this is an important factor in knowing the capacity you have to run your business.

When I was working four jobs, it wasn't ideal for me to take on 121 clients, as I was time bound and so financially it made more sense to offer group opportunities, so that I could earn more in less time and serve more people. That is exactly what I did. Time is money.

You need to also master money. How you track it, invest it, save it. Money management has been one of my biggest challenges personally and within my business and I am so passionate about helping with this too, as unfortunately we are never taught how to budget, and it is such an essential skill. Money management is about just that, knowing your numbers, your budget and always being clear on tracking that, especially as your business grows.

My recommendation is to always be on top of your finances within your business. Track what's coming in regularly, what's going out and be mindful of your expenses. My biggest mistake at first was an unwillingness to invest, because I wasn't making any money, yet it was the support and knowledge I needed to invest in, in order for my business to grow. You may find yourself in a similar situation, the chicken, and the egg. What comes first? Honestly, find a way. For me it was just going for it. I'm not advocating getting into debt but what I am advocating is finding a way.

Then there is the other hand with financial management, spending too much, which I have also done. Once I began investing it became like an addiction. I saw a return and was addicted to learning the next thing, spending on the next thing because I believed I needed it. Let me tell you, you don't need to learn everything right now and you don't need to invest in everything. It is about choosing what is right for you right now. This held my business growth back a lot, because whilst I was learning the knowledge I needed, I was unable to implement it all, leaving me in the time management trap again. It was also leaving my business below the baseline I needed to break even and earn a profit.

Let's face it, profit is scary. Managing tax and being self-sufficient, it is scary. For so long, it felt way safer for me to be on benefits and that held me back. I had to make that brave change to say no to investments I didn't need and start thinking smarter about what I was investing in and being intentional about it, and trust that the money I was spending was going to bring a return.

My biggest advice is to manage your finances. Know where your next client payment is coming from. Know when your next expense is to go out and make sure you retain enough cash in the bank to make those payments. It sounds simple, it really is, yet I struggled to maintain that basic level of cash flow and many clients have discussed the same issue with me. Decide to make this change.

At this point in my story, I have to touch on how this still recently affected me. In 2024 my business has already taken more money than any other year, which is amazing, but I have also spent a lot. I invested in a team, with a grant that I was awarded last year, which has funded most of the support I now have, however I wasn't ready for this level of growth and not only did it bring up some fears around money and management, it gifted some old money stories and behaviours, but I am now able to recognise these so I could work on it.

Writing this book has been quite an investment, in money and time, but I spent time stripping back what I really needed, instead of piling more things on my to do list and sabotaging achieving what I really wanted when the goal of a work life balance was just within reach. It's funny how we do that isn't it? So close to the success we desire and suddenly we sabotage it. I got to the point of recognising what I was doing and told myself no more and now I am on the way to huge changes in myself, my business, and my life. The book is being published, I am working less than I ever have in twelve years and I am about to begin launching in person events and potentially a whole new business in 2025. Watch this space.

The Production & The Practical

You hopefully should feel ready to manage your business and its processes better around your services, time, and money. I hope by now you feel equipped with methods that you can implement within your business which will productively move you forward.

It's time to produce your actual services with some practical action. Mind mapping is always a winner for me, but you can plan it as you like. List it, draw it, vision board it. Whatever way you do it, brainstorm ideas for your business for now and the future, distant and far. Spark your motivation and decide on what you're going to work on successfully selling first.

Once you have decided, practise focus within your marketing. Decide how your services will coincide with each other. This could possibly look like launching and opening up your services every month, with all of them running alongside each other. Mapping this out helps ensure that I am not only stacking my income with multiple offers, but also, I am able to manage my capacity between multiple clients in multiple ways of serving them. How will your services co-exist in your world?

The most essential practical action for time management for me was deciding upon my dream schedule. I coined this idea in 2023, and it really transformed my focus in a time where so much change could have easily had an impact on my time management and overwhelmed me. I have seen enough business owners go through it in my time and fortunately I have learnt from watching hard challenges others have faced and decided to be intentional with when I served my clients plus the other activities required within my life and business. It's not perfect, because perfection doesn't exist, so I just like to accept that things are as perfect as they can be over time. My advice is to set a vision of a dream schedule, where there are no limits and create one in your current reality that you can actually commit to now. Map out your week, by first making a list of all the things you need to take action to get by in life and business and compile it into a workable schedule.

At the time of writing this, I have just achieved my dream schedule, after seven months of tweaking and trying and testing and it feels amazing to have a balance after all these years. I am completing this book in Summer of 2024, having worked four-day weeks, and had additional time off with my children and enjoying days out, whilst still supporting clients, working on new projects, and attending a retreat, business events and meeting up with friends. If my future self could go back and tell my past self what I know now, it would have saved a lot of overwhelm. I am grateful for the journey I have been on though because I know that it was worth experiencing so that I could improve step by step and it has enabled me to share my stories with you and my strategies for managing when building a successful business.

Last but not least, I would love to direct you to my Organised Business Toolkit, which you can find within your book resources. This toolkit will help you manage money as well as other areas of your business. Set a time aside in your diary on a regular basis to master completing your bookkeeping. Trust me, having it up to date will save a lot of stress and overwhelm and it can teach you a lot about how your business is really performing right now too.

Chapter 8

Finance Fix

Revisiting Money Mindset & Dedication to Money Management

Following on from the regular action of updating your bookkeeping accounts, I want to reiterate the importance of money mindset for your business growth. First you must absolutely know and accept that having more money is possible for you. It may not have been a previous story that you have seen evidence of, but it can be. Look around at some of the most successful entrepreneurs that you know. If they can, you can. Decide now that it gets to be easy, it gets to be part of your reality and that you are committing to greater money management.

Here is what you should think about if money could talk:

- What would it say if it recognised you weren't keeping track of it?
- What would it say if you weren't spending it wisely?

- What would money say to you if you were talking to it negatively?

I am pretty sure money wouldn't be impressed by the relationship you have if you are in a place where you aren't committed to tracking it, enjoying it, loving it, and feeling gratitude for it.

This is the first place to start. Your finance fix is surprisingly not about strategy. You can manage money well but still be in a lack mentality around it. This is exactly what had happened to me in the past. I was actually earning money, but I was afraid of it, so instead I saved what I earned and paid for things I wanted on credit, building up debt. Most of us are guilty of it and it's so easily done, mostly because it is easy to accept that debt is easy to build. What if you decided that wealth was easy to build too? This is the biggest realisation, why not allow for healthy earnings, saving and spending. It gets to be the reality. This is often a challenge that needs to be worked at. I have always been great at budgeting, however my relationship with impulse buying and worthiness with money were poor. This resulted in a self-sabotage cycle until I recognised that I could change it and be in control of it. This made a difference to my life and my business.

As you have seen my journey has been up and down, but I eventually found balance. Nothing is perfect, but the work/life balance was getting easier and easier. I discovered that stepping into a new level, real growth comes from not only investing in my business but investing in myself.

You have been on the journey with me where you have heard my stories of building debt, building confidence, and working on strategies to get results, but what I hadn't been investing in was myself. Not my knowledge, not my business skills, but investing in my mind, my body and becoming a better version of myself. That began to change in 2023, when I recognised the connection between mind, body, and my business. Full alignment wasn't happening because my energy wasn't right and so I did something about it.

Unfortunately, we live in a society where we don't prioritise investing in ourselves to feel good. We may see the things you can see in physical appearance, such as nails and hair, but what about the things within you? How are you brightening up the things on the inside? I can dye my hair pink and paint my nails purple and feel damn great but it's only putting a plaster over the parts that need healing.

I hired a therapist. I jumped into an opportunity that would help with my leadership skills, my health, and my business all at the same time. I started investing in myself and not just my business and the result of the version of me that exists proves that therapy is invaluable. When it comes to money, I want you to be selfish, I want you to indulge in yourself and to buy the thing you want that will make you feel good inside and out. Do it in a way that holds duality of spending but also saving. Doing it without getting into debt but also without guilt. Energetically you want to enjoy and be grateful and feel into the excitement of getting your hair done, painting your nails, or going to therapy.

Budgeting and The Money Management

I have already introduced you to the organised business toolkit, where there are free resources that you can use for your money management. I learned a lot about money mindset and money tracking from my own mentors in the past and the money gurus that I followed online and suffice to say, everything I read, listened to, and practised paid off.

Let's look at your business budget. Do you have one? It's not always a common thing to have in place, but I always recommend it and not just in business either. Clearly understanding where all of your money is, bank accounts, cheques, debts etc. is the first step to getting a handle on it. Then you want to recognise where it is coming in and where it is going out. Only when you look at what you are really earning can you understand the gaps and how you can make changes to earn more. Only when you understand where your money is going can you really see what you are spending it on and if it's worth it. It gives you power to be super clear.

When I budget for my business, I set an 'allowance' on what I am willing to spend on areas of the business. This will change year on year, depending on my business goals. In 2024, during the time writing this book, I invested a lot into business events. I had attended many networking events before, but this was about getting into bigger rooms and making more connections. My budget for this was much higher than previous years, as I was writing this book and as a result of that, hosting my very first face to face event. I wanted to make new connections and build an engaged community around the launch of this book, to get it into your hands and help you build your business. I needed to be where other business owners were and network and that comes at a cost.

Other things in my budget are my team running costs, software running costs and essentials, such as my domain, website, Zoom and Canva. My business couldn't run without them at a bare minimum. I have a set budget for my own mentoring and training. Having a set spend per month for each area of my business ensures a minimum level of profit. It also ensures that I am not overspending and paying out more than I earn. This is a place I have been to before, which held a lot of embarrassment when payments failed, and I used to feel desperate for the next client payment to come in to cover pending payments. It is not an abundant place to be, and you want to practise your business budget from a place of gratitude.

Is it frustrating that my website platform and all in one system costs nearly £100? Yes, but I am very grateful for all that it allows me to do and the amazing customer service that the hosts provide, alongside the new and evolving developments. I now choose to be grateful for every outgoing payment as it provides me with the ability to run a business I love. All of these payments are an investment into the future of the business I am building. Once you see spending on your business as an investment, or as I have mentioned, spending on yourself, you can connect with the outcome you will receive, the return on the investment.

What about once you have stuck to your budget and retained a profit, what then? Good question. I feel there is not enough education on this area of finances, and I am by no means a financial expert and can only teach from experience but what I do know is that for eleven years I have been told to save for tax, I have been told to maintain capital and well, I never had. Part of me probably believed I would never be where I am today anyway, so I didn't need to save it. It also didn't feel safe, cue money mindset issues. Those gurus that recommend saving for those purposes are absolutely right and I realised this at the most difficult of financial difficulty, when those payments were failing and debt repayment reminders were hitting my email inbox, dropping via text and phone calls. Don't get me wrong, the bailiff wasn't at the door, but the hounding was enough to stress me out enough into taking action. It was tough, but not impossible.

From this place I put a blanket ban on investing in masterclasses, courses, online business resources etc. as I had access to a lot already but hadn't used them. I didn't need them and instead gave myself validation, which was a mindset shift.

If this is where you have been coming from too then I validate you right from the very moment you read these words on this page. I am not saying don't invest, of course I know that it's important, but what I cannot stress enough is that endless masterclasses and resources that you invest in are only going to put a strain on time and money. I do however advocate investing in bespoke support where you can access mentoring where and when you need it and it doesn't have to be constant, although I do admit that I like to have my own mentor accessible too.

In 2023 I was awarded 'Access to Work' funding to support me with my business, which is granted to support those with disabilities, health conditions, learning difficulties, mental health or neuro diversity and it took my business to a whole new level that I never expected to reach.

Whilst I was able to access this support and invest in my business growth, I shared my story on social media, gained load of interest as others wanted to access this pot of government money too. The issue is, typically it takes some effort in the beginning if you're not already established. I was approved instantly, but for those within the first year or not yet taking in any payments, a business plan and financial forecast is needed. This is exactly what a bank would ask for if you were applying for a business loan. Most people reacted to this stating that they don't have time, don't know how and one of my clients even said she 'can't be arsed'!

The thing is, doing this work will get a massive return on your time investment, £32,850 worth, in my case! When it comes to money, to creating plans and forecasts and budgeting for your business, I want to get real with you. If you cannot be 'arsed' to implement these necessary resources, then can you be 'arsed' to be successful?

Some real talk for you. The matter of fact is that less than 5% of people do what it takes to succeed, doing what 95% of people didn't, or couldn't be arsed to do. This is the difference between succeeding and reaching your goals. I wanted to talk about this because as you reach this section, based on numbers I know how it feels. It's facing up to reality, it's scary and in my head, numbers present a challenge. You choose how you respond to these icky situations that you're not comfortable with and can take responsibility for the result.

When we talk about money management you will see that mindset plays its part. The gurus are right, and you want to think about taking home pay, tax, and national insurance (if you're in the UK) and ensuring you have enough aside as running costs or future investments. I came across an amazing post on social media from a finance expert, quote 'Claire Sweet' where you take your earnings at the end of the month and take 55% for profit, 30% running costs and 15% goes in a pot for tax. When I saw this concept, it just blew my mind and changed my business money management game. It is so simple but effective. Now I will be honest, when I came across this I had just finished a £2K per month contract with a big client and so had a financial drop and had just invested in my team too, so my running cost were high and 30% wouldn't cover what I needed for the month ahead, so I adapted instead and I would recommend looking at your monthly earnings and adapting too. It looks something like this:

Monthly running business costs:

£100 for mentor
£50 website costs
£15 for zoom
£10.99 for Canva
£100 for VA
Total running costs £175.99

Business earns £2000 per month.

55% = £1100 to pay yourself
15% = £300 aside for tax
30% = £600 saved for running costs

Leaving a surplus of £124.10 per month, which can build up capital over time.

Doesn't this just make it simple? Yet we are not taught to do this! My biggest advice is to take this section and implement it. Analyse it, journal on it, process it, action it. I wish I had done sooner, because having money in the bank, even on lower cash months, really makes a difference and I love that it's easy. I am all for ease in life and business.

Take this as your sign to work on your money management if you haven't already.

The Price and The Process

One of the most common questions I am asked by clients creating a new service is 'How much do I charge?' I have been asked this by peers in spaces I have invested in, and I have even asked myself. There is no generic answer though. What I will say is, you want to consider cost and profit, but there are so many pricing strategies that I could write a book on those alone! The best thing you can ever do is to keep it simple. No matter the pricing framework you do go with, do keep it simple and always ensure that you are making a profit.

As you know, I am in a service-based business and so I thought I would openly share my pricing structure from my coaching qualification days. One of the first things I learnt was that group programmes are often a third of the cost of a 121 service and so that is exactly how I have priced my offers since. For example, my hourly rate at the time of writing this book is £200ph for 121, however it is discounted for larger packages. When pricing this, I factored not only the hourly time commitment, but also the time I would be committing to the client between sessions, to arrange sessions and to cover the running costs of being able to provide the sessions. My sessions require a Zoom subscription, my website host platform where clients access all their resources and my contract service, all which have a cost.

The one third price of my group session is £66, to reflect the fact that as long as I have three paying attendees, I am making my hourly rate and I feel comfortable in this price point because I know it returns a profit. I haven't always been comfortable charging this and it did take work and practise saying it and quoting it, not to mention that the feeling you have behind the price of your service is absolutely an essential part of the process. If you cannot feel like you can fully support your price point, and this holds you back from taking action on sales strategies or consistently offering discounts then this is potentially the mindset block you need to work around. Don't let the fear of charging for your work hold you back.

Fun fact, I never had as many clients than when I first increased my prices, and it was a dramatic increase at the time. I realised that the service, I provided was a match for these prices and I wanted to call in a particular client that took me, my business, and my service seriously and knew that the client's behaviour would reflect the price. Pricing based on who you want to work with is also part of the process alongside having to get comfortable with charging more.

In 2023 I went from charging £75ph to £200ph and increased the price on all my services. Why? Firstly, I was launching a new mastermind with experts who were charging a premium price as they are qualified experts within their field. I had to match that but also position myself in the market. Cheap prices can often be perceived as cheap results/services and that was definitely not what I wanted to represent. I also decided what I was no longer available for clients who weren't behind investing in their growth, committed to taking action or who used excuses as to why they were not successful. Setting that intention changed my mindset and my reality with results following. The client who pays £60 for a one-to-one session will show up differently to the client who pays for the £150 session. Currency is commitment. Again, it's no coincidence that when I increased my prices my clients were showing up and getting better results. Think about this in terms of your pricing and whether 'being affordable' is a value that serves you well. In terms of being the client, how have you shown up for your investments?

Fix Your Finances

I'm sure that from this chapter you will have taken something that you need to take action on, even if you are a 'Savvy Sally' and you are on top of your money management, this is your reminder to check in with your finances and see where changes can be made.

And remember… take action!

Start recording your income and outcome monthly at the very least! Check in with your mindset around money when you are dealing with finances, remembering to have gratitude for your expenses.
Practise pricing comfortably whilst also ensuring profit. This may be your action to revise your current service prices.

Here is where I advise you to do what I did when I approached this part of my journey, step into being a leader, not for others, but for yourself. Lead yourself better with money, lead yourself better as your business manager, lead yourself better before you lead anyone else.

A lot of my story has been about my money challenges and my story is so much more than this, as it's not just about the money, it is about time, freedom, and happiness. However, it is money that pays my bills, gives me opportunities and as much as I am the down-to-earth approachable mentor (as quoted by my clients) I am absolutely in it for the money too. I don't want to work for free. Just as at the same time I value my clients, my service, and the experience I offer. This didn't come naturally, and I absolutely had to step into leadership. In the past I was calling out clients for investing in many things and mastering none, I was judging behaviour, I was expecting better, without coming from a place of doing better myself and I had to do the mindset work and financially literacy to change that and instead lead myself to master, to improve my behaviour and to raise my expectations of myself, before judging anyone else.

Chapter 9

The Sales, The System & The Success

Clear Core Offers

You may have heard this advice before and it's not a cliché, it's just true and the sooner you put it into practice, the sooner you see the results.

Choose ONE thing to sell, be really good at it, sell it really well and then add in your other offers.

The creative within me massively struggled with this. I would happily create something new every day if I could because I just love making stuff. The reality is, there is so much more to successfully selling something than just creating it, we have to market it too!

It begins with a clear offer in the first place. When you are marketing to the world how you can help them and calling people out as your ideal clients, it must be clear what, why and who you offer this service to.

I already touched upon your product suite earlier in the book, but now I want to go deeper into building a core offer suite and how that can contribute to the success of your business.

Imagine you are just starting out; nobody knows you exist. If you show up on social media every day and introduce the many different things you can do, will people buy into that? No. A confused mind always says no. It also takes a lot of building authority and credibility, especially building a business online these days. It is essential to create multiple touch points when you are sharing what you have to offer. People need to see what you're selling again and again and again…so with this in mind, I recommend creating a clear core single offer that you can energetically get behind. Something that potentially has the greatest impact for you financially once you fill your spaces, as this can create a baseline income and anything additional you sell on top of that is a bonus. If you are consistently selling and focusing on one thing, then energy flows where focus goes, and money is simply an exchange of energy.

The service you choose can be anything you want. For me, in 2024 that was my Sustainable Sales: The Mastermind, because I am absolutely passionate about what I have created and I know it can impact businesses owners if they tap into having all bases covered, which is what this programme offers, with a focus on building a business that sustains consistent high cash income on a monthly basis. I know that having clients within that gives me a great baseline income and if I focus on building that it can really increase the profit my business has. This ensures that anything else I create in future can just stack on top of that. This is where building your income streams comes in as having multiple streams just adds an extra layer of stability within your business.

Once you sell something, your big, exciting offer and you sell it well, add another in. This is where you can build a foundation of clear core offers, so that when your people come across you, they know exactly of the ways in which they can work with you.

This is exactly what I have focused on in the past year (2023-2024), as I had done the work on building the foundations and getting very clear on what I wanted to serve and who I wanted to work with. At this point in my business, after much trial and error, which we all go through, as I have so openly shared, I got focused on what I was delivering and became consistent with this. Selling my 121 spaces, Sustainable Sales Mastermind multiple times per year, knowing that I would re-open my Foundations programme again this year and then I introduced Organisation Implementation, my mini mastermind. I had four core offers within my service suite, of which three I mainly focused on selling, as I was already at capacity for my 121 services. Having this focus on just these offers brought about a lot more ease within my business, as I could rinse and repeat content and strategies that were working. This is exactly what I did, which saved me so much time, but also helped me earn more money on a consistent basis, so behind the scenes I could focus on writing and creating this book.

Sales System

The sales do not come without a system in place. Simply put, you need to know the exact actions you are taking to ensure the sales come in. I know this throws up some money mindset and icky sales feelings but in short, you're going to have to get over those thoughts and feelings if you want to be successful. This is why I covered mindset in the very beginning. If you have got this far and you're not ready to push for the sales, you desire then I recommend going back to chapter two and revising it on a regular basis until your subconscious overcomes your fears to allow you to take action.

Everything I have spoken about within this book is foundational to your sales system, that should be clear at this point. The way you consistently work on your mindset, the branding you inject into everything you do and the way you lead yourself on your social media, ensuring visibility and the rest.

All of it contributes but, in this section, I am going to introduce you to the basics of having a funnel in place.

Step one: Awareness
People don't know you exist unless you create awareness. This applies to your offers too. Your ideal clients won't know they exist unless you create that awareness. An important part of your sales system should be to generate

leads through creating awareness of who you are, what you do, the problems you solve and the services you offer.

Step two: Desire

This is the next phase, when someone is aware of the above, but they are not sold on it yet. You need to warm them up. Often this is provided through giving value, by creating authority with your brilliant testimonials and building credibility through showcasing your expertise. These actions build desire to get the result that your clients have, what you can offer as a solution and to work with you.

Step three: Action

As stated, this is where your dreamy clients are sold, and they take action. If the process involves a freebie they are signing up for, they hand over their details in exchange for your value. If it is a service, they pay you in exchange for a solution to their problem. Action only happens when your ideal client is aligned with what you offer, and they are clear that it is right for them.

The three parts of your sales system should happen as part of an ecosystem and not only one part existing at any one time. You will find that your followers, your email subscribers are all at different stages within the three-step funnel and so you need to continue to keep the cycle going to funnel people through, by creating awareness, creating desire, and offering an option for these people to take action.

3 step

Process

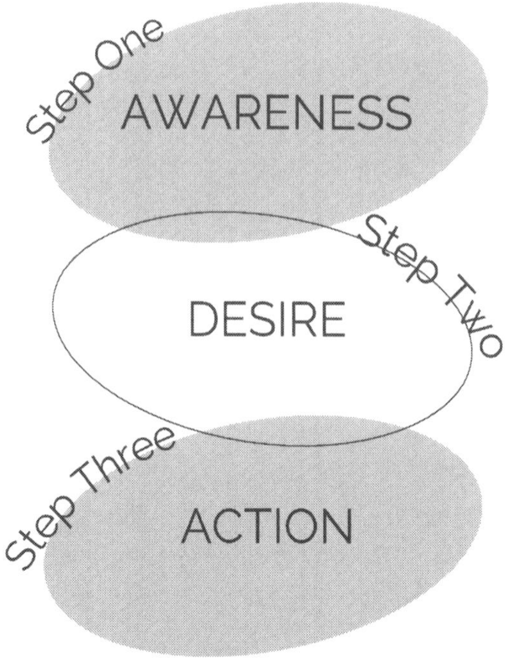

At the time of writing this chapter of this book I had just sold out my Mini Mastermind: Organisation Implementation and when the last client joined, she said she was so grateful that she had seen my post on social media offering that last place, otherwise she would have missed it, and she hadn't seen anything about it. The thing is, in eight weeks I had posted at least once, if not more, every day on my Facebook group, page, profile and my Instagram about it. I then shared stories regularly on both platforms and sent out emails to my list with it mentioned at least twice a week. Here lies the evidence that you can never talk about something enough, as it can be missed and so you must create awareness.

Referring back to how essential your brand is to your overall sales system, as one of your many foundations, building desire can only happen when your marketing speaks to your ideal client directly, where they are at in relation to the solution you are offering, especially with a key service. It is consistently something to be worked on.

As I began year three of my business, I had a realisation that my new services were not a match for my audience. I had a high number of leads, but I hadn't been using my content to give value to the topic of creating balance through better business management and operations, which my next level clients needed and not the initial work on getting the sales. To build desire you have to know your client thoroughly and communicate to them through your content marketing. I knew that my next level client for my Sustainable Sales mastermind was already earning, and they didn't need the sales strategy secrets shared on social media, they needed the management hacks to save time and allow them to streamline and create growth. Only then when I communicated this, did selling my signature offer to those next level clients become easy. Your whole energy of your sales system needs to be a match for what you're selling at the given time.

There needs to be an action to take. Your dream clients cannot take action if an opportunity isn't presented to them. We have already established that always creating a synergy between awareness and desire is important, but just as equally as it is to also share sales posts, share what you are selling, follow up and ask for the sale. Without your action they cannot act.

This part of my journey is almost where I am at right now. In 2024 I am celebrating consistently making a stable income and investing in a team too. I am just about to gain myself two new qualifications that fully align with the direction I am taking my business, and I couldn't be happier. That's the biggest and best win of all for me, happiness.

As I write this, I have just texted a business friend about how this summer I found a great balance between work and having time to spend with my family. I absolutely love working so my dream is not to work less, but to have the balance of both, because it makes me feel good. This is my exact goal for you too, to find your way that works for you.

Getting back to the sales talk, all of the above only came into fruition because now more than ever I have taken time to research and get to know my audience, what they want and what they need. Understanding where people are at and supporting them to navigate is important to me, but even better, it gets results when you research and apply. Diving into the needs of the people you need to be communicating with and using your findings within your marketing and when planning your services is so powerful. Focus on the features they need but also the transformation they desire to achieve. This is exactly how I sold out my new mini mastermind recently, because I researched and applied.

Sell Even More

I love a sales strategy and the best thing about when your process is working and your core offer is selling well, you can add in even more. This is where you can create the magic of stacking those offers and creating multiple streams of income and it gets to be easy with these simple strategies.

1.Increase prices

If your core offer has been selling well then, it's time to increase profit now that you're not new to the game. Those low prices and beta offers should only exist for so long. If you're finding that you're fully booked, then it's time to increase your prices! This will help you to earn more, rather than sell more. The beauty here is you then may sell more but still earn more, so you're actually working less to earn more. It is the most obvious strategy when looking to increase income. However, this isn't always the case. On occasions, increasing the price can increase perceived value and you may find it attracts more clients. This is something that happened for me with my 121 services. When I first began, I was charging £40 per hour. I never sold a single session at that rate! When I increased it to £60, they started selling, clearly because the higher price was aligned for me and the value to my clients. I now charge £200 per hour (with reduced rates for packages), and I have had more 121 clients right now compared to when I began three years ago!

2.One-to-many

Everyone is savvy these days and it is another obvious strategy, yet a lot of business owners are fully booked at 121 and not prioritising time to implement a group service. The reality is your income is capped if you stick at one to one and if you're looking to grow then it is wise to work on bringing in a one-to-many model. My biggest tip for implementing this well, is allowing yourself to sacrifice time and make space for it so that you can bring your new group offer into existence, otherwise it's just not going to happen. You need to create the space to enable yourself to fill it. Creating a group offer is a popular option and in order to hit the spot for you ideal clients, it will take redoing much of what we have already worked through, in terms of research and your brand message around that one service, in order to connect with the right people and successfully sell it.

3.Upsell /upgrades or add-ons

You are 60 to 70% more likely to sell to an existing customer than you are a brand-new lead. These statistics have power and offer a strategy that you don't want to miss out on. If you have gone to the effort to generate a new lead, build desire and they are taking action, clicking your link, and buying from you, then this is a great opportunity to offer a greater service and make more money.

Disclaimer, this only works if the offer aligns with what the customer is already buying. Imagine you are signing up for a group programme, but it doesn't begin for another four weeks, you're excited and would love to start straight away, as you're paying a pop up appears to add on a workbook to download that can get you started with solving your current problem and it's a bargain, it's less that your current purchase, it's a no brainer so you add it on. This is where those small offers start to passively generate additional income. When you have set up your payment systems, links, web pages etc, ensure that you fill gaps with an upsell.

Think about how you can offer an additional service for the client to add on. If not an add on, could you add an upgrade to the current offer? For example, if they are buying a group programme with you, could you add an upgrade to VIP and offer 121 sessions alongside the group programme? The client who is excited to get started and solve their problem is bursting to get more from you and it's your opportunity to help them.

4.Bundles / packages

As you build your product suite you may find that you have a lot to offer, and clients may want to pick and mix the things you have available. This is where creating bundles and offering a small discount can entice clients to buy more. Have a look at what you can bundle and package together within your product suite to offer even more value and ensure your client has everything they need.

When you are looking to grow your business, you want to ensure that you can implement new income streams and create more, without working more. Think about how you can do this? When I was launching this book, it was definitely going to cost quite a lot of money, more than I knew I could get on a return on investment when selling the book. The investment was over £1000 and yet this book is selling for less than £15 per copy. Unless I had multi-millions in my audience, it's highly unlikely I could return that investment instantly. This is where I began planning how I could use this book as a tool to generate leads and also bring in some cash when I host my book launch event. The event itself is £500, just to attend and eat. I wanted more though. I had a vision of creating the best goody bags my attendees had ever gotten, giving signed copies of my book, and coming together in a beautiful venue, but it all costs money. I thought about how I could cover the cost of all of this with very little work. First things first, I decided I would charge for the tickets and ensure they covered the cost of food and the lovely things I wanted to include at the event. Then I offered the opportunity for other businesses to sponsor the event. This went extremely well and brought in £525 for very little work, which helped get them visible and supported me to provide a roller banner for my event, buy the author copies of the book and the gifts that I wanted to give to attendees. The sponsorships sold out within days! This shows how much of an impact an additional income stream that you can implement without working more can have.

Magic in the Method

This is where the organisation of the sales system comes in. Once you start deciding upon your core offers, after much brainstorming, notes, research (definitely do your research!) it's wise to create an 'offer brief.' This comes in handy if ever you hire a professional copywriter, content creator or experts to help bring your creation to life. For starters though, create it for yourself. It is great to save and refer to as you write sales pages, social media content, including sales posts and to ensure you have the overall key points behind your offer message.

Within your brief, ensure you include what the offer is, what it does, who it is for, what the features are, the benefits and the promise it delivers, the pain points it touches on.

Now that your offer is super clear, it's about mapping out that three-step sales process. Thinking about how you are consistently generating new leads and creating brand awareness, who are you reaching and where, what are the strategic actions you are taking to be visible? Then once you start building an audience, decide where you are directing them to and how you are going to nurture them. Your aim is to build desire as your people begin to get to know you and in order to do this you need to show up and give value. How are you consistently going to nurture and give value?

Finally, no sales strategy is complete without the actual focus on sales. Selling somewhere, at least once a day, every day should be a priority for the growth of your business. Think about the strategic actions you can take on a daily basis to encourage sales to come in? Sell where your ideal clients are, sell to your audience, market in different ways and in doing so, be intentional. Simply putting a post on social media is not a strategy. Everything within this book, the vision you have, the goals you are working towards, the operations, the process, THAT is the strategy.

The magic happens when you can operate your business from a place of organisation and showing up regardless of circumstances, achieving a full balance between work and business. I used to believe it was impossible, but this year I have mastered it in a way that feels right for me, and I want that so much for every other business owner too. This summer I have spent working three days per week, reduced by one day and being able to go on days out and enjoy time as a family, without it impacting the work I need to do. I have even managed to edit a book and write a 2000-word chapter to contribute to another book too!

None of this happened by accident, I created it. Method in the madness is literally my life, there is a method to everything so I can stay on top of workload, without getting overwhelmed and without it impacting my sales and my income. Decide today that you are going to make that change. If you are currently feeling amongst unorganised chaos, decide now that this will change, so that you can find balance and harmony of working and living life, no matter the circumstances you're in.

Chapter 10

Marketing Master

Daily Method of Operation

Well, I couldn't write a book without mentioning this, could I? Those that have witnessed my mentoring journey from the beginning will know that this is where it started… and I'd love to share with you how it came about.

Back in my keepsakes business days, I had left my job, had baby number two, and decided to give this business thing a go. I decided it wasn't going to be a hobby anymore. I wanted to make money. One of the tips from a leader in one of the MLM companies I was part of, advised setting up a business breakfast network meeting. So, I followed her advice. I initially hated it but with my ability to use the power of social media I managed to gather some business owners in a Starbucks meeting room. Over coffee, one of the women told me how she realised that some Facebook groups had rules for promotion, and she gathered them into a list and used it daily to promote her business. I went home, I trawled through all my groups, joined loads of new ones, and made my list. Every day I then started posting in them. Over the next few months, I stopped hosting those breakfast meetings, mostly because the networking felt uncomfortable as a 22-year-old mum, new to business and judged because I was part of an MLM, at the time 'trying' to sell FM perfumes. I say try, because I didn't do very well at all, spending more than I earned. I was also judged because I didn't drive. One of the attendees stated, 'How can you run a business if you don't have a car?'

So, I decided to do things my way, without a car, building online and I joined some free online business focused classes and talked a lot about social media. I took notes on everything, had ideas, felt inspired and I added to my list. The more I learned, the more I added to my list. It went from being a group list to a daily checklist and I started getting sales.

An opportunity then opened up to run the 'Mums in Business' Leeds networking group. My business was starting to make traction and I thought this could only boost it, so I applied, got the role and dived right in. One month later, I was more confident going live and started sharing my hacks to grow on social media and at that point earned £1000 in the month from my keepsakes business and for the first time I had £600 profit!

Remember the DMO the one that kick-started my business?

That was the beginning of *The Queen of Business Organisation* and I have come far since that day but what is bittersweet is that whilst I reflect on that time and complete this final chapter with you, I have made a promise myself to build community and connections like that again. I have decided to go back to basics with what worked with me in the past and bring business back to a place of building genuine connections. Of course, I am a genuine person, you take me as you see me and I am who I am, but as business had grown a lot of connections have been lost. It's not intentional, it's just that as you grow you focus energy where the money is and actually focusing attention on building community and connections will flow back to you. At this stage of my business now, I feel ready to lean back into that and I do hope you will be part of the journey.

The DMO, let's create yours. It's a to-do list you use every day, but unlike a regular to do list, it's never complete. It's a list that you rinse and repeat. It consists of income producing activities. The activities I list on mine are to generate new leads and grow my audience (Facebook group and email list), nurture people in my existing audience and connect with them and selling; any activities that intend to sell. I broke my list into the group list I mentioned in my start up story, details of the services I would be marketing and then my daily, weekly, monthly, quarterly, and yearly tasks that keep my business running. The tasks then became about the efficiency of running the business and operating in a way that got things done without overwhelm and it works!

I have a couple of resources for you:

1. A free 'Daily Method of Operation' video inside your book bonuses.
2. An income boost bundle, which has a DMO template, training videos and so much more. It's not free, but as one of my readers you can have it discounted. You can also find this within your book resources.

Enjoy!

Email Marketing Mastery

Email marketing was the thing I didn't know I needed that contributed to my success landing those five clients on day one. An email mastery course was the very first big investment I made into my business. At the time I paid a beta rate of £200 for a course that is now 10 x that price. The tech wasn't easy, but I loved it! Statistics say that for every £1 you invest into email marketing you get £47 back! That's a brilliant return on investment in my opinion, but I've never actually paid for my email list, and I definitely get a return!

The best thing about email marketing is that you can start for free. I highly recommend Mailerlite as a starting point because it's easy to navigate and offers more on the free plan. Most people are now savvy when it comes to email marketing, they know the structure of it; sign up for a free thing, get a series of emails and then be enrolled onto the regular email list, receiving weekly newsletters or updates.

Here's the thing, mastering email marketing can offer so much more than just one lead generating freebie. I highly recommend this method of bringing people to you but there's so much more that email marketing can automate and do for you:

- Sales sequences when launching something new.
- Automate removing those who are not opening your emails.
- Send out follow ups after a purchase.
- Send out sequences after specific actions.
- Onboard new clients.
- Offboard clients at the end of contract.
- So much more.

Imagine the time this could all save you! Think about how you could use email marketing to automate, save time and grow your business.

I always say that there's never anything you *should* do for your business, except this. You don't *have to* use social media to grow your business, you don't *have* to show your face, you don't *have* to do dancing reels, but what you definitely *should* do is have an email list. It's also not enough to have one existing, but also to send out regular emails. My top tip is to send at least once per week. Most business owners will opt for once a month, but the reality is, that's not enough. Imagine you posted only once per month on social media, who would remember you existed? Definitely email out more than that, bi-weekly at first and build up to weekly, if not more.

I know that you worry about your ideas, it's another piece of content to prepare each week, but here's where it gets to be less overwhelming; just repurpose your social media, blogs, website, or other content. It gets to be that easy!

A final note on email marketing is to just give it a try. Don't let the tech scare you off. We live in a world where YouTube can teach you almost anything and if not, I do have an easy step-by-step email course. Just get started and make sure you don't set it up and forget about it. Get your email marketing working *for* you and your business.

Notice how effective sharing my story with you has been? Sharing your story is massively beneficial to your business but also to your ideal clients. The chances are that you are supporting them with something you have personally overcome yourself and so they will want to hear your story, your challenges, and your triumphs. Share it all with them to create relatability, especially within your email marketing!

Level Up Your Launches

Ah launching, another big scary thing that business owners find their head in a spin over. That doesn't have to be you because you've got me!

There are many ways to launch a new offer, and neither is right or wrong but those that work or are trending do change over time, it always depends on the current behaviour of consumers, so it's worth knowing who your ideal client is!

Three years ago, launching during a five-day challenge was popular but then people stopped consuming them and most people, myself included, reduced it down to a three-day series and these are often done live. These days they're not as effective as they used to be. Often, I have noticed that a lot of marketers launch at the same time of the month. As a consumer I found it overwhelming as I signed up to all the challenges that promised to change my life, then for the business owners, it's a lot of competition and work to keep the audience's attention.
Like I say, there are many ways to launch, and I could write a whole book on just launching, however I want you to know the important parts of leading a launch for your shiny new idea.

First of all, whatever you're launching doesn't have to be new. A lot of big brands go hard on a new launch of a product that already existed. An example is McDonald's, initially this brand was a barbeque restaurant in the early 1940's later transitioning into focusing on their best-selling product - burgers. Over time their logo adapted too, from a plain black and white name to the golden arches that we all recognise today. The arches became visible in 1961, chosen for its ability to stand out. The brand adapted over time and introduced the colour green, to highlight the launch of the efforts of the brands aim to work on environmental sustainability. The business has existed for decades and was still selling the same products, but now it is well-known for the fast production of burgers but launched again with a campaign of sustainability. Often as your business evolves you will find colours, images and values change, just as it has for McDonald's and researching their history makes me feel better about my also ever evolving journey.

Launching keeps things fresh and new, bringing zest to your existing product suite. I couldn't write a book about business without also mentioning another iconic, recognised brand, such as Coca-Cola. The brand is recognised around the world. The company has one of the cleverest marketing teams, with the unique launch ideas they have. Remember the flavoured colas that they launched? Cherry will always be my favourite, but these launches over time were clever! They launched flavours, often for a limited time, which created a desire from consumers and increased the demand. A scarcity tactic to get you to stock up and try their new flavours, but the strategy behind the launch didn't end there. One of the best methods of marketing is word of mouth and because the flavours are often so unique, people talk about them, and it does the selling for them. How many times have you tried food or drink based on recommendations? Trying out fresh and new things can get your brand talked about.

Finally, I want to shed light on launching evergreen or cart closing. Evergreen is when you launch something and it exists, you can sell it all the time, at any time. For example, a course that anyone can join at any time of the year. The opposite is when marketers decide to launch and open the cart for ten days and then close. Often the door won't reopen for a particular amount of time and the strategy involves bonuses to entice people to buy during that open cart period.

These are pretty much the done ways of launching and what most marketers will teach you, but along with those five-day challenges, the world evolves, and I believe quick launches are becoming a thing of the past. People are a lot savvier now and so they take more time making purchase decisions, they do research and often need more warming up. It's no surprise, considering the rise in coaches, mentors and social media guru's that claim to solve all your problems.

A lot of very big industry names do still launch this way and with huge visibility and years of building and growth they have authority, so it works. If you're not quite there yet I definitely believe it pays to pace yourself with your launches.

In 2023 I launched with a live series and had no interest at all. Had I stuck to that two-week launch, it would have failed. At that moment in time, I adapted and continued to talk about it. It was October and I wasn't planning to begin the programme until January anyway. I introduced an online workshop and I talked about it every day over the next three months and sold out all ten spaces by Christmas! It was my first fully sold-out offer and I believe the way I moved through the launch, with creativity and adaptability allowed for it to work. I made £8000+ off that launch, a result I had never had before, with previous launches hitting £1500 to £3000.

Fast forward six months, as I write this chapter, I have just used the same method to launch my Mini Mastermind: Organisation Implementation and again, it sold out! This time the launch was a lower investment and only brought in £2220 but I sold all the ten spaces that I desired to sell.

From both these launches I learned that longer launches can work and they're easier! I also discovered that talking consistently and adding more points of contact for your audience to see your message around what you're selling, in different ways, is very effective. You can never talk about what you offer enough within this fast-paced world.

What about outside of launching? There is absolutely a place to make more money without launching. I am currently celebrating making passive income, after initially doing work and then having sales come my way without needing to do anything. This feels like the lazy girl way of selling, but I absolutely love it! Passive services are things like my instant access downloads and master classes or courses. Think about what you can sell completely passive by creating once and selling again and again.

Lead Launch Convert

I hope you feel an abundance of steps closer to being a marketing master.
The final process I want to talk you through is leading your ideal clients, launching your services, and converting those leads into paying clients.

I've touched on lead generation already, but it's so important, which is why I'm mentioning it again. Leading your ideal clients is not just about how you can attract them into a Facebook group, onto an email list or be a number on a spreadsheet. It's also about the way you communicate with them before selling to them, to communicate a message that's clear. The biggest missing piece I see with any marketing is that one day you may decide to launch a new service and without planning, warming up or much thought, you put it out there. I'm not saying this won't work, but it's highly likely that your audience isn't ready yet. Here's where you instead lead them in.

Content is the absolute king of marketing. To be an online business owner in this century is to be a content creator. Everything is content! Used intentionally, your content can start to build awareness and connection with your ideal clients, based on everything your brand encompasses and also in relation to the service you're about to launch. Bring your topics into your content before you launch it and create a no-brainer when you launch because you have already led people in with the awareness and value you have created, through your content.

When you launch, don't give up at the first hurdle. It sounds obvious but if you really want your offer to sell, then you need to get it out there and talk about it non-stop. Focus on visibility and sales content. There is more than one way to sell, so be open to opportunities and talk about it consistently. I often notice that business owners plan a launch, go all hellfire at first but after a few days and no interest, just stop. Never stop. You never know where your next client could come from, and people are always watching. I have shared enough stories here that teach you this. Launch your new thing and talk about it like it's the best thing since sliced bread, because if you're passionate about it, then it is! Talk about it, talk about it, and talk about it even more. People need to know it exists!

Finally, I want to help you convert more! Whatever it is that you're selling, there are always ways to increase conversion.
The key thing is to think about buyer experience, what can affect this before the clients buy? Personally, I absolutely love automation! If I'm buying something online, I love to know what's happening next. Yes, you can put this in place, but that's after the sale, so how does it help convert more? Well, tell your audience what the process looks like before you sell. Educate on what the next steps would be, so your clients know what to expect.

Insights
Such a great tool on all platforms these days. If you're not utilising these then you're missing a trick. Take a look at your insights on social media, for your email list, website, and other platforms. I track mine every month, so I can see overall how my business is performing. This type of analysis helps determine where focus needs to go and what my next steps need to be so that I continue to grow and increase conversion.

Social proof

Improve your chances of securing the sale by always sharing testimonials, client wins and feedback. I'm definitely a screenshot junkie and ensure I collect every positive thing my clients say, because it's great to use for marketing purposes and you are sure to convert more if people can actually see the results of your great work.

Be sure to go out there and DO your great work. Let people see it, experience it & grow your business!

Most of all, when you are launching, selling, or focused on your business growth, always ensure that what you do is aligned and right for you, for your business and you do it your way. I didn't write this book to overwhelm you with more and more to learn and do (although you may feel that's exactly what has happened!) I wrote it because I want you to build your business foundation, get organised and streamline your operations so that you can find the ultimate work life balance for you, which leads to better health, better wealth, and better happiness.

At the time of writing this chapter I am about to go into a new week where I get to go out and celebrate my wedding anniversary with my family, then enjoy taking the kids to soft play the next day, following that with a bowling game and time in the arcade and finally, going to a retreat where I have no work and no family or life distractions. I love that I have been able to build this, and it won't impact my business. I love that I can go away for the weekend and still earn money, I love that I can come back to work the following Monday and pick back up where I left off. I love that it has now become easier than ever.

None of this is 'luck.'

None of this happened by accident.

None of this was offered to me.

I made it happen.

So go out there and attract those dreamy clients, build beautiful relationships, and make some money but do it in a way that feels right for you, with balance and abundance.

Final Chapter

A message To You

As the journey I have shared with you on these pages comes to a close, I wanted to share some cliché quotes, because I love them but they're also true. So here are my final thoughts for you to take away…

Just F*cking Do It!

Nobody else will do it for you. It's up to you. I hope you picked up this book as the first step to taking action. Now go and take the next step. I know you want to succeed, and I also want you to. This is my message to you to just go and f*cking do it. Take action. Don't allow excuses of others holding you back. You are in the driver's seat and here is me giving you permission to take control of where your journey goes.

Take Messy Action!

Oh, we make mistakes sometimes, don't we? I have shared some with you, here in this book. I have been open, honest, real, and raw. I wanted to show you the reality but also it serves as a reminder that nobody knows what they're doing in the beginning. We have to learn. It means that you will get things wrong, but you find a lesson in that and move on. There's no such thing as failure in my world. So, whether you feel you can't because you don't know how or its not perfect, do the messy action anyway. You will learn along the way.

Dance Like Nobody's Watching!

This is exactly how you should show up as you grow your business. Release all judgement from anyone because nobody judges you more than you do yourself and when you work on that you can put on your best performance. Make big moves and find your own beat because your rhythm is unique and that's what will bring music to the ears of your dreamy clients. Go out and get them by dancing like nobody is watching and be true to you.

You've got this. Your song is on.

Dani x

The Queen of Business Organisation

-Dani, The Queen of Business Organisation ♛

I wanted to offer more than just a book. So here it is, a selection of resources, as referenced throughout the book.

Scan the QR code with your phone camera to access.

Facebook: Dani Louise Smith
Instagram: @queenofbusinessorganisation
YouTube: @queenofbusinessorganisation
Podcast: www.queenofbusinessorganisation.co.uk/podcast

www.queenofbusinessorganisation.co.uk

Acknowledgements

Who do I begin to thank for this business journey? It's the hardest part for me, for fear of missing anyone out. I will begin with my clients, past, present and those to come in future. I am so grateful for you all. I truly wouldn't be here without your trust in me to support you.

To my headline sponsors, Leah Palmer, author and Samantha Hyam, course creator and consultant, who supported my book launch event. The support this has offered to get this book into the hand of business owners is much appreciated.

To my amazing teamie, Sharon Hadley, at Sharon Hadley VA Services, who was one of my very first mentoring clients and now I have the pleasure of having you on my team. I am thankful for your help with bringing this first book project to life.

To Lisa Williams, my choice for a book coach, to support me with making my vision happen, my vision board dream, inspired by you, the Vision Board Queen.

To Louisa Herridge, my proof-reader and editor, of course becoming my very first reader.

To Denise Duffield-Thomas and her books, the only ones I will re-read cover to cover, and, in all formats, which have contributed to a growing money mindset and chillpreneur lifestyle.

To Leona Burton, founder of Mums in Business International, the first place I found myself and where anyone knew who I was, which also inspired this journey to become a mentor.

To Ward 19, LGI, especially Julie, you don't know how much you all had an impact on my confidence and belief in myself.

To the mentors I have had over the years. Steve Carroll, a volunteer and first ever business mentor, within The Prince's Trust when I launched my very first business and began my journey.

Mandy Nicholson and your money mindset story, which inspired my journey. Danielle Hobson, as my very first mentorship investment, who supported me to do more than 'make an extra few quid' as I first set out to do. Samantha Hearne, as my 2024 mentor at the time of writing this book.

To my Mum, for stating that you 'knew I would do it' when I told you in the pub one day about wanting to publish a book. I borrowed your belief in me.

To my children, Stephen, Archie, and Eliza, for the number of times they had heard ‘just one minute’ whilst I focused on something work related.

Last but not least, to Daniel Smith, my husband for making everything I do possible and supporting me, you are my right arm and I appreciate you being there through the blood, sweat and tears and never allowing me to give up. You have been there through it all. Love you x

About The Author

Dani Louise Smith is *The Queen of Business Organisation*, a business mentor supporting holistic and wellbeing service-based business owners and coaches to earn more without working more. She has run three successful businesses and overcome adversity. After a tough time battling her mental health throughout the 2020 pandemic, Dani went on to build successful businesses in the handmade creative, networking, and mentoring industries. Her experience in business organisation and succeeding in extraordinary circumstances has helped to shape her into a strategic, honest, and down-to-earth mentor who isn't afraid to dream big for herself, her family, and her clients.

In just six months, after closing her handmade business, Dani transformed her life from debt to financial freedom, after changing niche and helping many women to begin successful entrepreneurship. Dani has a consistent presence across most social media platforms and an ever-growing podcast, 'The Sustainable Service Based Business Podcast.'

Dani is a huge believer in going after your dreams and that it all begins with a vision and a plan. She is an advocate for mental health, disability and inclusivity awareness and is known for her unique story online.

Dani lives in Leeds, West Yorkshire, UK, with her husband, three children and dog but mentors online as well as in person.

Printed in Great Britain
by Amazon

48516370R00106